FRAGMENTS
of MEMORY

FRAGMENTS
of MEMORY

A NEPALI NATIONAL'S REMINISCENCES

SATISH PRABASI

GREEN PLACE BOOKS | *Brattleboro, Vermont*

Printed in the United States

10 9 8 7 6 5 4 3 2 1

Green Writers Press is a Vermont-based publisher whose mission is to spread a message of hope and renewal through the words and images we publish. Throughout we will adhere to our commitment to preserving and protecting the natural resources of the earth. To that end, a percentage of our proceeds will be donated to environmental activist groupsand The Southern Poverty Law Foundation. Green Writers Press gratefully acknowledges support from individual donors, friends, and readers to help support the environment and our publishing initiative. Green Place Books curates books that tell literary and compelling stories with a focus on writing about place—these books are more personal stories/memoir and biographies.

GREEN
PLACE
BOOKS

GReen
wrITers
press

Giving Voice to Writers & Artists Who Will Make the World a Better Place
Green Writers Press | Brattleboro, Vermont
www.greenwriterspress.com

ISBN: 978-1-7336534-0-4

THE PAPER USED IN THIS PUBLICATION IS PRODUCED BY MILLS COMMITTED
TO RESPONSIBLE AND SUSTAINABLE FORESTRY PRACTICES.

Dedicated to:

Lekhnath Upadhyaya
My late father, for his love and foresight.

Sheila Prabasi
My soul mate and life partner for fifty years.

APPRECIATIONS AND GRATITUDE

I would like to extend my appreciation and gratitude to all those who have helped me in giving a shape of this memoir. This book had its genesis on a cold, snow covered January in 2017. My daughter Sarina had arranged for us to attend a week-long writing retreat in Vermont. Hence my first and foremost gratitude to Sarina for her creative determination in pushing me to write this book. Equally, my wife Sheila has provided me unflinching support throughout the process.

Sincere thanks to Steve Eisner, the spirit and moving force behind the When Words Count Retreat and to his capable team. I appreciate Asha Hossain for her design of the book cover and Peggy Moran for the initial first edits of the first draft. Mr. Saroj Sharma, whom we call Rajuda, gave valuable support to me and Sheila during various phases of our stay in the Netherlands. Our heartfelt thanks to him. Ms. Dipika Shrestha provided invaluable technical and editorial support in completing the manuscript. My deeply felt appreciation and gratitude to her.

Dede Cummings, publisher of the Green Writers Press encouraged me as a Judge to complete the book as well as supported me by agreeing to publish this memoir. Her familiarity with Nepal and deep knowledge of Buddhism was a constant source of inspiration to me. Last but not the least, John K. Tiholiz and Jennifer Young improved the text by meticulous editing and helpful suggestions and observations. I am obliged to them both.

It is obligatory in Nepali cultural tradition to thank teachers and gurus who have inspired and given intellectual support. Accordingly, I wish to appreciate all those who provided me inspiration and guidance during my long journey of search and quest for the meaning in my life. There are too many of them to mention here, however, I must express my gratitude to three of them: Professor K.K. Shah, a Kashmiri scholar from Banaras, Jan Tinbergen, the famous economist who was deeply committed to global development, and James Grant, the visionary director of UNICEF. Their critical support has been the springboard for my learning and evolution as an activist. In the formative years of my life in Nepal and India, a number of extraordinary ladies have helped me, to some of whom I must extend my appreciation: my second sister Satyawati, my aunt Subhadra Sanima, and Sarala Upadhyaya, the sister of my wife. I can't imagine the course of my career without their continuing support at critical junctures in my life.

I feel lucky that I knew and benefitted from the three extra ordinary administrators of Nepal. They are unsung heroes of the then-kingdom. It was my pleasure and privilege to get to know them and obtain their crucial support as and when needed. I recognize them for their vision and foresight: Devendra Raj Upadhyaya, Krishna Bom Malla, and spiritually enlightened Mr. Kul Shekhar Sharma. All of them deserve a full-length analytical biography. Hopefully someone will write about them in the future.

During my professional life in Asia, Africa, and Europe, I was blessed to get to know some of the outstanding people and personalities. Furthermore, I had the privilege of enjoying their friendship. They are too many of them to list them here. I must however mention some of them who impacted me in various ways. They are: Dudley Sears, the founding director of Institute of Development Studies (IDS), the U.K., Lady Hicks of Oxford, Hans Ollman of International Cooperative Alliance

(ICA) of London, Dr. Surendra Saxena of the U.K., Eric Jacoby of Upsala University, Sweden, Bapu Deolalikar of India (currently living in Maryland), Mr. Mani Sharma of Nepal (currently living in Pennsylvania), Late Dev Bhalla of Leiden University, the Netherlands, Ms. Ida Van Zunderen of the Hague, Nailton Santos of Brazil, and Dr. Ramon Harmano of the Philippines.

My special thanks to my son Samir for introducing me to the huge continent called Australia. The vibrant city of Melbourne and the academic ambience of Monash University will always remain fond memories.

PART I

CHAPTER 1

EARLY MEMORIES

THERE was hushed expectation and a sense of trepidation, too. It was a dark, cold January night in the Himalayan foothills of the village Govindpur. After the death of two girls and three boys, the woman was about to deliver another baby that night. She was mortally afraid. What if the baby was a girl and not a boy? The master of the house was pacing outside on the veranda and praying silently to his Hindu god, "Let it be a boy." The village midwife was at work within the dark, smoke-filled room, and finally she gave out a shout of joy: "Malik! It's a boy! I deserve a reward." There was a round of joyous clapping at the happy news. That boy was me.

I may be one of the very few persons from South Asia still alive to have lived through and imbibed lessons from both a feudal, almost stagnant social system and a fast-moving, internet-based, data-driven society. When I grew up in Nepal, there were no paved roads, nor was there electricity in the entire kingdom. It is recorded by the British government in India that in 1940, the Nepalese prime minister's first car was dismantled and carried in bits and pieces into the mountains by 28 porters to be reassembled in Kathmandu Valley. The fuel for that car came at the courtesy of the British authorities in Calcutta; it was also carried by porters. From that almost medieval milieu of Nepal in the early 1940s through a lifetime's quest for new experiences spread over 68 countries, I reckoned that the two most persuasive women in my life, my wife and my daughter, might be right: I have a story worth telling—if not for myself, then for future generation of booklovers like me.

Thanks to the geo- strategic location of Nepal, with China to the north and India to the south, I have been blessed with unique opportunities in my life. I am convinced that, had I been born 60 miles to the north of my village, I would be herding yaks and sheep on the Tibetan Plateau. On the other hand, had I been born even a few miles to the south, I would be singing religious hymns in praise of the goddess Sita and Lord Ram in India. I credit the geographic accident of my birth with greatly improving my prospects. As I was coming of age in the post 1950s, Nepal was opening up to the wider world.

I have been able to meet world leaders, writers, and other notable people throughout my life. Had I been born among the two billion souls north and south of Nepal, those meetings likely would have been impossible. I remember with pleasure meeting with Deng Xiaoping of China; Madam Sun Yat-sen (she corrected me and said she preferred her birth name, Soong Ching-ling); and Indira Gandhi—one of the most powerful female leaders in Asia, if not the world—at the Pugwash Conference on Nuclear Disarmament in Tamil Nadu in 1976. I met Henry Kissinger in the Great Hall of the People in Beijing; the mountaineer Tenzing Sherpa on our way to Bhutan; and Sir Edmund Hillary, the New Zealander who, with Tenzing Sherpa, first summited Mount Everest, in New Delhi in 1953.

Another distinct blessing was the faith showed in me by Jan Tinbergen, a development scholar who would become the first recipient of the Nobel Prize in Economics. He recommended me for a scholarship to study in the Netherlands in 1965. I had the pleasure of meeting the bicycle-riding Queen Beatrix along the sand dunes of the Scheveningen beach. Though I cannot claim to be a dispassionate analyst, I venture to record my life experiences as a South Asian man who has seen both the feudal culture of Nepal and the political transformations—and upheavals—of the twentieth and twenty-first centuries.

These fragments of memory encompass my experiences in Asia, Europe, Australia, and the United States. I have not attempted to write a comprehensive memoir; instead, I record only that which struck me, shocked me, or gave me a sense of pride and pleasure. Memories of my childhood in Nepal, followed by my studies in Banaras (Varanasi, India) while living in the household of my sister, have been very educational.

And as a young traveler, I was fascinated by the richness and variety of European cultures. The first question I was asked was, "Are you a Gurkha?" Gurkha soldiers were renowned for their valor and fighting spirit, especially amongst the British. Once, when I was a student in the United Kingdom, an ophthalmologist treated me without charging me a penny when he found that I was from Nepal because he recalled fondly that he owed his life to the bravery of a Gurkha solider in Malaya when the guerilla rebels were fighting against the British in the 1950s. The twelve years I spent in Western Europe (two in the U.K. and ten on the continent) were some of the best and most formative years of my life.

My time in the United States and my contradictory experiences there have been summarized in the later chapters of the book. The United States has been an extraordinary land of competing extremes of ideals and cruelties. My Brazilian friend at the Hague, Nailton Santos, used to say that America is the only country founded by people imported from other lands. In this day and age, when immigration has become both a political and a social issue, I find great hope in this country's capacity for compassion and regeneration of human values, a capacity not seen in other countries. I believe the U.S. is right to claim that it is exceptional. But it is also true that exceptionalism has branched out in many directions, highlighting some undesirable human traits. My introduction to the people of the United States began early in my life. The first and most remarkable American I met was my boss and friend, John Holiday, a black Republican from the South stationed in Nepal as the deputy head of the United States Operations Mission (USOM). He gave me deep insight into America's nobility, but also into the crushing injustices imposed on the country's black population.

In my teaching days in the Netherlands, I had no qualms about shouting slogans alongside my Dutch friends: "Hey, Hey, LBJ, how many kids did you kill today?" But I did not refrain from praising the freedom of the press in the U.S. when the crafty Richard Nixon was dethroned by two journalists working for *The Washington Post*. My French friends used to say, with envy and admiration, that only in the United States would a president resign because of "one minor fault." In France, the two young journalists would have suffered an accident, like a car crash, and drowned in the Seine.

As I reflect on my life of learning and questing, stretching over seven decades, I am struck by the interplay between historical forces and individual wisdom or folly. I am both impressed and dismayed by human emotions and instinct, and my view of human history suggests an ebb and flow in the stream of human affairs. My study of ancient history has convinced me that there is a pattern of progress followed by decline in human civilization. Based on my own life experience and reading of the violent events of the twentieth century, I often ponder the eternal question that continues to confound historians: "What if?"

During my early years as a student in Banaras, my Marxist friend, the Bengali Dada, took me to a memorial rally a week after Stalin's death. We were assembled, I vividly recall, in a huge park called Benia Bagh. Tens of thousands of grieving people were there, most of them carrying portraits or small photos of Stalin, and hundreds of them wept loudly as though a member of their own family had died. Comrade Satin, a popular politician and eloquent speaker, addressed the gathering. All of us were numb with sorrow at Stalin's death.

But a few years later, Nikita Khrushchev's famous report to the Soviet Central Committee on the extent of Stalin's atrocities against his own people hit us hard. The gory details were published in the newspapers and repeated on the radio for several weeks by the Voice of America. I recall the intense discussions we had in student circles about the veracity of this news. Many of us blamed the CIA for propaganda. In those days, we used to talk of planted news, not "fake news," the term made so popular by the 45th president of the United States.

When I went to Western Europe, the fervor of the Cultural Revolution in China had taken firm hold of intellectuals and students alike. I remember that my African and Latin American friends and I used to visit the Chinese embassy in the evenings for discussions of the little red book, *Quotations from Chairman Mao Tse-tung*. Over cups of tepid tea and unfiltered Chinese cigarettes, we used to discuss the originality of an agrarian revolution as opposed to an industrial one. Marxist theory posits the beginning of revolution by industrial workers and their organizations (such as unions). Mao pioneered the theory of revolution by poor peasants in agrarian society. Since many of us came from developing countries with a mainly agricultural base, we were intrigued and attracted to this new approach of development. Our Chinese friends glorified the Cultural Revolution. Little did I know then that more than 30 million Chinese people had perished, human offerings to the doctrinal holy words of Mao. The little red book turned out to be a harbinger of endless tombstones in the People's Republic of China.

Our family lived in a compound of thatched-roof houses. The biggest building faced east and had a spacious veranda that wrapped around it. The small structure to the west was our kitchen, called "*bhanchha ghar*." It was located somewhat far from the other buildings to avoid a fire leaping into the rest of the compound, thus causing a tragedy. It was prudent planning, except that in the rainy season, it became difficult for the members of the household to go there without an umbrella. A small building to the south was for storage, and another small structure to the north was our *puja* room, where religious ceremonies and daily worship and prayers were conducted. In Hindu and Buddhist traditions, north is considered auspicious because it is the direction of Lord Shiva and the sacred Mount Kailash. Countless religious pilgrims and yogis venture to the northernmost passes of the Himalayas in search of learning and enlightenment. I remember my father's two instructions for the *puja* house: take off your shoes before entering the room, and wash your hands before touching the books or offering your prayers.

In the middle of the village of Govindpur, there was a large pond—called a *pokhari* in Nepali—which served multiple purposes. The water stored there was used to put out the occasional fire sparked in an outdoor kitchen and spread by dusty gusts of wind during the dry season. Water from the pond was lifted by makeshift bamboo hand-pumps to flow down small channels, irrigating the vegetable gardens around all the homes in the village. In contrast, the rainy season caused problems of excess water and flooding, affecting many houses. Groups of families used to get together as a community to drain the excess water.

Each vegetable garden had, at the very least, some green chilies, a patch of potatoes, and some onions. Some vegetable patches were more elaborate, but these three plants were staples in every garden. During the lean season in the summer months, most villagers had a breakfast of puffed rice, *muri*, with chopped onions and chilies. Farmers from the surrounding area would come, sit in our courtyard, and eat before they headed to work on my father's fields.

The northern footpath led to a famous temple two miles away called Bhagwati Mutth, which my father visited every day. It was a shrine to the goddess Durga in her incarnation as Chhinnnamasta, proudly wearing a garland strung with the severed heads of the devils and demons she had destroyed. Young children like me went to Bhagwati Mutth on the many festive days of celebration with which the Hindu calendar abounds. We enjoyed outings to the temple because it was a source of entertainment and excitement.

The southern dirt road led to the villages of North Bihar, India. The road was used most frequently by men, women, and ox-carts trading in kerosene, salt, oil, sugar, and other essentials. It was the busiest dirt road in the area surrounding my village.

My mother always tried to overfeed me; I called her Aama. My father, Lekhnath Upadhyaya, whom I called Baba, was a remarkable personality. He was called "*Malik*" by the villagers. He was a man of small stature with ferocious energy. A kind person by nature, but with flashes of anger—a person with an acute sense of fairness and justice to the poor. He would joke and talk more gently with me than anyone else. I was very proud of him and in awe of his personality. I was particularly close to Baba; I loved and respected him. As my parents' only son, I was adored and pampered.

In those days, justice used to be administered by the headmen of villages. There was no legal administrative system, so the administrator of each district assigned the task to village headmen. My father was the village headman, known to be harsh yet fair when he dispensed justice. In this capacity, my father used to dispense justice in minor cases. Murders used to be referred to district headquarters, to the office of *Bada Hakim*.

I still remember an incident that occurred when I was five years old: a farmer had grazed his herd of water buffalo on another farmer's field. The animals ate up all the newly grown rice crops. The farmer was caught with his buffaloes and brought to Baba to decide the appropriate punishment for his transgression. Many villagers came for the spectacle. Baba sat on his wooden bench, smoking his favorite hookah.

He asked the accused, "Were you grazing your animals on his field? And if so, will you repay this man with an amount of rice from your crop?"

The foolhardy farmer denied it vehemently: "I did not graze my animals on his land."

Baba turned to his favorite helper, Belua. "Bring the bag of chili powder and a bucket for milk."

CHAPTER 2

MASTER SAHIB

NEPAL, nestled between India and Tibet in the foothills of the lower Himalayas, was a Hindu kingdom tolerated in its independence by the British. Proud home of the highest mountain, Mount Everest, Nepal claimed to be the land of the brave, and the homeland of the world-renowned Gurkha soldiers. We Nepalese have always been proud of our independence. The mountain people from the north descended to the malaria-infested southern lowlands in search of timber, oilseeds, and legumes, and they gradually colonized the strip of land called the Terai. Baba was one of the people who came down from the western hill village of Jhiltung, and over the years he acquired a hundred acres of land near the border with India. He called this piece of land "the abode of Govinda," or Govindpur, named after Vishnu, the Hindu god of prosperity.

In January 1940, when I was born, Nepal was still an isolated, closed, and repressive society, afraid of outside influences and uncertain of its own direction. The Second World War had started in Europe, but most Nepalese were blissfully unaware of it. Thousands of Gurkha soldiers joined the British army to fight British wars, but Nepalese civilians were denied the right to travel abroad without the privileged permission of the Ranas. In those days, the King of Nepal was not powerful. The Ranas were the ruling class of Nepal, and they held absolute administrative and judicial power from the office of the prime minister down to that of the chief district officer. Nepalese citizens from the Terai region had to get a stamped entry – permit called *radhani*, stamped in order to enter the capital city. Those who wanted to leave the city had to obtain similar authorization.

There was no system of high-school education in Nepal. Against this repressive background and suffocating social system, Baba decided to hire the services of a resident teacher to educate all the boys and girls of the village.

The teacher was a memorable personality named Nageshwor. We affectionately called him Master Sahib, the word *sahib* being an honorific. He was a tenth-grade student in the northern Indian state of Bihar who had given up his studies to follow Gandhi's Quit India Movement. Quite successful at first, the movement petered out after a few months, leaving tens of thousands of students suspended from schools and unable to continue their studies. Nageshwor was one of them. He then started walking toward Nepal in search of employment and came to Govindpur. He asked the locals if there was a school in the village and where he could contact the head teacher. They laughed and said there was no school for many miles around. He should go and talk to the *zamindar* (landowner), who had a young son and was in search of a teacher.

As luck would have it, Baba and Nageshwor met, liked each other, and our village got a live-in teacher who later doubled up as our local health provider.

As a young teacher, Nageshwor started to instill a sense of health and hygiene among the young boys and girls. I remember our shock when he insisted children must come into the classroom, which was the earthen veranda of our house, only after washing their hands and feet. He also insisted that each student buy a slate so that we could write. The parents protested the extra costs at first, but eventually they obliged.

Nageshwor's presence in our house brought about my education, that of my five sisters, and that of tens of other village girls who otherwise would have remained illiterate. In Nepali society at the time, girls were forbidden to read and write. It was believed that providing reading and writing skills to women was a great sin. My mother, a god-fearing woman, was denied the chance to write the Nepali Sanskrit alphabet. As a young boy, I was astonished to hear her recite many verses from the holy books, notably Nepali versions of the *Ramayana* and the *Bhagavad Gita*, without ever having read them.

Nageshwor also started a few physical exercises, which led to much amusement among the kids and bewilderment among the parents. Gradually he won everyone's affection.

Since education was restricted in Nepal, there were no published textbooks. Master Sahib traveled quarterly to Indian markets in his home state of Bihar to select books appropriate for students in various grades in his veranda-school. He would also bring notebooks, colorful pencils, geometry boxes, additional writing paper, and other education aids. If the journey to Bihar was eventful for him, his return to our village was an occasion for joy and celebration for all of us children. Thus, a system of reading and writing developed in our village. The flip side of it was that we knew more about Indian heroes and history than Nepali ones. We became more proficient in Hindi, the language of our books, than in Nepali, our national language.

Master Sahib held an annual festival, Saraswati Puja, with prayers and celebration for the goddess of learning. On these occasions, there would be a community-wide undertaking to erect a *pandal* (a special platform), install a statue of the goddess, and create an arch made of green leaves and young banana trees.

In 1949, on Saraswati Puja Master Sahib announced terrible news to us. He said that he would no longer be able to teach us, as he already had imparted all his knowledge and skills.

"Remember," he said, "I am a tenth-grade dropout from a school in Bihar. I therefore do not think it is right to continue teaching you all beyond that grade. I am sad, but all of you have to find your own ways and means to continue your further studies, if you wish to do so."

This created panic in many households, including mine. Baba flared up at Master Sahib, almost shouting at him, "How can you discontinue teaching? We brought you to this village to teach our children; while staying in my house, you also became a local doctor providing basic health care to all four villages surrounding Govindpur." After a lot of arguments and counter-arguments, it was agreed by the village elders that Master Sahib would not teach the elder students but would continue teaching the younger children who had not yet reached seventh grade.

This created a problem for me. Where should I continue my studies? My mother was adamantly opposed to my going to Kathmandu, even though I could stay with our relatives. She insisted, "My Sanobabu (little son) will surely fall ill in the harsh, cold climate and unhygienic conditions of Kathmandu."

Our teacher also said that Kathmandu was out of the question, since "The young one has studied books used in Indian schools. He will regress if he goes to Kathmandu."

My second sister, Satyavati, who was visiting our parents in Govindpur from Banaras, had a suggestion: "Sanobabu can come to Banaras. I will look after him as well as our mother does. And my husband is a homeopathic doctor, and he will make sure that my brother does not suffer any serious illness."

It was the month of *Ashwin* in the Nepali lunar calendar (corresponding to September or October). Baba had decided that I should leave Govindpur to study in Banaras the following month, *Kartik*, when Hindu and Buddhist pilgrims light cotton-wicked oil lamps. Lamps signify the arrival of light to diminish, if not destroy completely, the darkness and ignorance. It is believed to be the holiest month to dip in the Ganges and to seek blessings at the temples in Banaras. My father wanted me to reach the city in time to experience the ceremonies and gain blessings in such an auspicious month.

Once the decision was taken to send me away, my mother started crying. But she also began cooking and preparing goodies for me to take to my sister and dry snacks for our journey. I tried to console her, telling her "Aama, it's not forever; I will be back!" Deep in my heart, I was also torn between the excitement of living in Banaras, of which I had only heard stories from my sister, and the unspeakable fear of leaving my father.

"Why don't you come along with me, Baba?" I asked him several times.

His eyes would get moist, but his answer was firm and always the same: "You need to be educated. I cannot leave my land, my farming, and all my responsibilities here. You will come back, I know, during your holidays."

I couldn't understand it. On earlier occasions, I had always been able to persuade him for the things I wanted. Yet this time, he was adamant and said, "It is only for you. You will know when you are older."

In retrospect, I admire his clarity of purpose in assigning the highest priority to my education. I now realize that I emulated his example in my own life by giving the highest priority to my children's education.

After much heartache and with tears in his eyes, Baba hugged me, bid me farewell, and wished me a successful journey. He also gave me a little piece of paper and said I should read it after I reached Banaras. My mother was so overcome with grief and was crying so much that she remained inside the house. And Master Sahib hugged me vigorously and said loudly, "Please make your parents and me proud." Thus, my lifelong journey, my quest, began at the age of ten.

Some memories of childhood remain fresh as ever: I distinctly remember, so many years later, my first journey away from home. Baba could not accompany me, so he sent a trusted chaperone with me. One early morning, we started out on an ox-driven cart for a seven-hour journey to the nearest Indian railway station, called Nirmali (the name denotes a clean and beautiful place, yet it was my first experience of a dirty town).

My father knew the owner of a Brahmin inn, so we rested there for the night. After getting down from the oxcart, I was shown a relatively clean room. The moment I entered the room, I heard a loud, ungodly noise, which sounded very close. The room seemed to shake.

I rushed back out to the front and asked the owner, "What is this loud noise I hear?"

He smiled and said, "You have never been to this town, so you don't know; it is the hooting of the railway engine signaling that it will leave soon for another station." Recognizing the confusion and innocence on my face, the owner kindly said, "I'll ask one of my workers to show you the station and the railway track." It was my first introduction to a mode of transport not based on animals like oxen or horses. The industrial age finally caught up with me at the age of ten. That black engine looked so huge and monstrous, but I could not believe it could transport over a thousand people.

The sights, the sounds, and above all, the overpowering noise of my train journey from Nirmali to Banaras overwhelmed me. The Indian train system was not well developed in those days. Together with my chaperone, I boarded a narrow-gauge local train that stopped at every station to pick up passengers. At each stop, a multitude of hawkers selling tea, snacks, and other items shouted to promote their wares. I was curious about everything that was for sale, though I had no idea how much anything might cost. I had no need for money in our village and had never actually bought anything. Even for such a long journey, Aama had supplied me with enough food for a whole family.

The train stopped at Samastipur, a junction whose name means "abode of abundance." Here, we had to change to a wider-track, regular-sized train that would take us to Banaras. A train-ticket collector came and stamped our ticket; I didn't understand why our tickets had to be stamped again, since they had already been stamped at Nirmali, but I kept quiet and handed over my ticket when he asked.

I was amazed at how crowded the train was. I had never seen so many people in one place in my life. The porters along the platform were even trying to push passengers and their rolled-up travel bedding, called *gunta*, into the train through its windows because the entrances to the carriages were packed. There was great confusion among people fearful of missing their train. I almost fainted; I felt suffocated by the odor of so many human bodies crushed together. Twenty-four hours after leaving Nirmali, we reached the Banaras cantonment, a station built for the movement of British soldiers.

Tired and sleepy, we got off the train and were immediately surrounded by dozens of porters offering to help us with our luggage. Suddenly, I recognized the familiar figure of my brother-in-law. I felt an immediate and tremendous sense of relief.

My sister lived in a locality called Brahmaghat, along the steps down to the River Ganges. With a wide smile, she looked radiant as she stood in the doorway greeting me with a lit oil-lamp, flowers, and incense. I touched her feet, as was our custom, and she introduced me to her mother-in-law, a beautiful, graceful woman with striking white hair, whom we all called Mua. She put her hand on my head and blessed me. I entered my new home away from home.

My first night away from my parents, before I went to sleep, I took out the piece of paper Baba had given me, opened it up, and read:

There is no happiness for him who does not travel, Rohita! Thus, we have heard. Living in the society of men, the best man becomes a sinner. . . Therefore, wander!

The feet of the wanderer are like the flower, his soul is growing and reaping the fruit; all his sins are destroyed by his fatigue in wandering. Therefore, wander!

The fortune of him who is sitting, sits; it rises when he rises; it sleeps when he sleeps; it moves when he moves. Therefore, wander!

I recognized the famous story of the god Indra, the lord of arts, dance, and music, from the Vedas. Indra encourages pilgrims to travel to distant lands. In the Atreya Brahmana, Indra, protector of travelers, encourages a young man, Rohita, to pursue the life of the road.

CHAPTER 3

THE CITY OF MANY NAMES

THE ANCIENT CITY of Banaras in Northern India has the unique distinction of being known by three names: the Hindu name, Kashi, which means "the luminous city of light;" the geographic name, Varanasi, since it is located between the rivers of Varana and Asi; and finally, in popular and colloquial terms, it is often called Banaras, a term coined by the British for ease of pronunciation.

When the American author Mark Twain visited Banaras during his journeys around the world, he observed, "Banaras is older than history, older than tradition, older even than legend, and looks twice as old as all of them put together."

From ancient times, Kashi, the luminous city, was renowned as a center for learning and scholarship. Many saints and philosophers lived in Kashi. Two of the most prominent are Shankaracharya, the founder of Indian philosophical system called Vedanta, much appreciated by the German Indologist Max Muller, and the English Philosopher Aldous Huxley. A noted poet of Hindi language, Tulsi Das, lived his entire life in the city of Banaras. He translated Sanskrit volumes of Ramayana to Hindi. His Hindi translations are chanted across Northern India even today.

The astrologers and priests and *pujaris* of Nepal's prime minister's court were trained in and recruited from Kashi. The ruling class of Nepal, therefore, had a soft spot for Nepalese students going there to study. Little did they realize that hundreds of students migrating each year from Nepal to Kashi were interested not so much in Hindu scriptures as in the English language, history, and politics. This is best illustrated by the fact that three Nepalese prime ministers were educated in Banaras and belonged to radically different political factions, ranging from radical communism to loyal monarchism.

In those days, I was too young to comprehend the social complexity of the Nepali community in Kashi. As I lived there longer, I began to realize that there were distinct groups of Nepalese people in pursuit of different ambitions. The first group consisted of scholars of the Sanskrit language and religious studies. Some of them were sent to Banaras for education by the rulers of Nepal so that they could be hired or appointed as priests, gurus, or astrologers depending upon their specialization. The second group consisted of retired Gurkha soldiers. They were veterans with disabilities, some of whom were lame and unable to walk. The third group in the Nepali community consisted of poor hill men who came down to Kashi in search of employment. Many of them worked as *paaley*, night guards. Their honesty was highly appreciated by the householders though their pay was meager. Many of these hill people used to work two jobs, becoming night guards and part-time workers as restaurant cleaners. Finally, there were young students, full of vitality and differing visions for their country. Some of them were affiliated with the democratic Gandhi–Nehru ideologies. Others were aligned with the Marxist ideology and committed to building a classless society in Nepal. They participated in student body elections and organized small meetings and rallies in favor of their candidates. I was attracted by their energy and skill in discussions and debates. Much later I realized that we were pursuing a mirage of building a Communist society where even the rudimentary base of industrial development was non-existent.

There was also an active group of politicians (some of them exiled from Nepal) who were intent on the overthrow of the Rana regime by fair means or foul. This group of politicians was centered on the personality of Bishweshor Prasad Koirala, an internationally known socialist figure.

I visited Kashi again after joining UNICEF as the Regional Planning Officer in Delhi. During this period, I realized that Kashi in the early fifties was very similar to Paris, the City of Lights, immediately after the First World War. Paris was then teeming with Russian immigrants of all kinds: White Russians, literary Russians, Russian dancers and artists, and those who wanted to overthrow the Communist revolutionaries in their home country.

Similarly, Banaras in the early fifties was teeming with Nepali writers, editors, businessmen, and revolutionaries adhering to different ideologies. There was even a Nepali dancer famous all over India called Sitara Devi, who could be compared with a famous Russian ballerina living in Paris.

Kashi helped produce four colorful prime ministers of Nepal. Most prominent among them was B. P. Koirala, the first democratically-elected prime minister. Krishna Prasad Bhattarai, a devoted follower of Koirala's, lived three blocks away from my sister's apartment. Manmohan Adhikari, a trade-union leader from eastern Nepal, later became the first Communist prime minister of the kingdom. He is ranked as the most honest politician, and, consequently, he lived almost like a pauper. Surya Bahadur Thapa was the fourth prime minister who had studied at Banaras University. He was a monarchist intent upon increasing the power of the royal family. Even at my young age, I used to speculate about how one university could produce students of such different convictions and ideologies.

I hold strong memories of Banaras for a different reason. The city of Sarnath is located some six kilometers away. Sarnath is historically famous as the town where Buddha offered his sermon to his first five disciples. Having read two books on the life of Buddha in Banaras, I was fascinated by the city. The first one was called *Life of the Buddha*, written by Ashva Ghosha. The second, *Siddhartha*, was written by the famous German author Hermann Hesse. I therefore used to visit Sarnath as a student on a rickshaw— the cheapest and the most private form of transportation in those days. In my early years of living in Banaras, Sarnath was a peaceful Buddhist city with many temples and stupas with quiet parks and lovely domesticated deer and antelopes roaming around. The Buddhist monks and lamas in their maroon robes walked quietly in and around the park. I was deeply impressed by the serene natural surrounding of this place. From my childhood I knew that Lord Buddha had delivered his first sermon here.

CHAPTER 4

THE DEATH OF A CHILD

UNIQUELY AMONG the cities of world, Kashi holds the distinction of being the place where people go to die. It is believed by the Hindus that if you bathe in the Ganges and live and die in Kashi, you will attain *moksha*, liberation from the cycles of birth, death, and rebirth. Because Nepal was a Hindu kingdom, thousands of aged men and women, some widows or widowers, came to live in Kashi. In fact, there is an idiom, "*Kashi baas*," which means, "going to live in Kashi until one's death." Neighborhood after neighborhood is densely populated with old Nepali widows living out their lives. During my four years of study there, it was believed that over 50,000 Nepali families lived in Kashi in pursuit of liberation of the soul.

After six months of living a student's life, I was told by my Nepali friends that many families had come to Kashi in search of the basic goods for survival: rice, bread, and clothes. Many of the men worked as night-guards protecting the mansions of the emerging middle class of traders and businessmen. The women worked as maids, street sweepers, and cleaners. They were the *lumpenproletariat* of Nepali origin in Banaras.

There were two unsung heroes who introduced me to this segment of the Nepali community: one was a man named Laata Dai, and the other was a woman named Amir ki Ama (the mother of Amir). They left a deep impact on my life and my worldview. Laata Dai was a tall man with Mongolian features, clear almond-like eyes, and shining, silvery hair. He had the upright posture of a military man, though he had lost his left leg below the knee during the Second World War. After his discharge from the army, he could not go back to his mountain village in Nepal because of his physical disability. Some of his Gurkha friends suggested that he should settle in Kashi, where he could get a part-time job and healthcare from one of the city's charitable clinics. He came to Kashi, and it was my good luck that I met him one morning at my brother-in-law's homeopathy clinic. My friendship with him opened a dark window for me on the poor and poverty-stricken people living among the lanes and by-lanes of the holy city.

Amir ki Ama had a stunning impact on my life—even on my name. She was a stout, hard-working, healthy woman of the Rai tribe of eastern Nepal. Her husband had served in the Indian police during the British Raj. He was killed during an encounter with Indian revolutionaries—*Kranti Kari*, according to Amir's mother.

This young, illiterate mother of a nine-month-old boy did not know how to return to her village in Nepal. She was helped by some women at the police station, who gave an address in Kashi. It was a dharamshala, a shelter for the religious poor and pilgrims, where widows and orphans could live for a limited time. Thus, she lived in a Nepali dharamshala for a while and she came to work in my sister's home.

A visitor to Kashi was struck by the view and acrid smells/aroma of the burning ghat. The most famous among these is Manikarnika Ghat, where I had spent my lonely hours as a young student. Professor Diana L. Eck has vividly described Manikarnika Ghat in her book, *Banaras, City of Light.*

Amir's mom worked part time as a housemaid and cleaner in seven households. If she found that a family liked children, sometimes she would bring Amir to her place of work. Other times, she went alone, completing her duties and rushing away to another assignment.

My sister's apartment in Brahma Ghat was child-friendly, so Amir's mom often brought Amir there. He was a bright young boy with mischievous eyes. When I was 11 years old, I used to play with him often because I used to be at home preparing for my school admissions exam and had time in the afternoons. I loved Amir for his innocence and extroverted personality.

One afternoon, Amir's mom came alone to our apartment. She was extremely agitated and told me with folded hands, "Bhai (brother), you have to help me as there is no one else. . . Amir is very sick for the last few days. I went to Birla Hospital with him, but they wouldn't admit him unless there is a male guardian."

I asked her, "Why did you take him to Birala Hospital?" In the Nepali language, cats are called *birala*.

She replied, "It's not a cats' hospital; it is a charitable hospital for poor people who can't pay fees to the doctors. I am told it is run by a very rich businessman."

Suddenly it dawned on me—it must be the hospital run by the Birla family, well-known all over India for his astute mix of business, religion, and philanthropy. I remembered India's great leader, Mahatma Gandhi, was murdered at a temple maintained by the Birla family in New Delhi. I readily agreed to go with her the next morning and be a guardian to Amir.

Later in my life, I understood that it was a medium-sized hospital. But that morning, it appeared huge to my eyes, and full of sick people crying in pain, spread out on the dusty and dirty ground floor. I was suddenly reminded of the young Siddhartha, before he became Lord Buddha—how he had wondered, why do people suffer pain? Why do they die? Why is there so much suffering? The middle-aged nurse showed some papers written in Hindi to me and said, "Please sign here." I did, and doing so, I absolved the hospital from any liability. Amir was admitted to the emergency room and given an injection and a couple of tablets, and Amir's mom was given some dietary instructions.

She was told to take him home and return after a few days. On our way home, I was struck by the change in Amir's mom's face: where there had been worry and despair, there was now a brightness.

I became curious about the life story of Amir's mom after our visits to the hospital. She told me that her real name was Sudha, but as was customary in rural Nepal, her husband began to call her Amir ki Aama (mother of Amir). They were very proud of their son and had big dreams for him. They wanted to give him a university education in India so that he could be prosperous and rich. He would not have to work as a hired farmhand on other people's land as his parents had done before coming to India.

With Nepal being a mountainous country and amid the hardships of life imposed by the hills, the caste system evolved in more practical directions than it had in India. In India, the upper caste, the Brahmins, and the warrior class, called Kshatriyas, observed a vigorous lifestyle. In contrast, in Nepal, with less facility for water and fuel for heating the house and cooking, the human settlements adapted to geographical hardships. Thus, the Brahmins in the hills and mountains of Nepal adapted Hindu traditions to suit the land. For instance, Brahmins were forbidden in India to plow their land, but in Nepali society Brahmins were obligated to cultivate their fields—the only rule was that they should purify themselves in the month of August by taking a dip in the river, wear a new religious thread called *Janai*, and chant a few prescribed mantras. This would take away the sin of plowing the land. This ceremony was called *Janai Purnima*.

I heard my sister and her mother-in-law grumbling that Amir's mom had not come to work. It had never happened before. Using a typical feudal Nepali idiom, they agreed that "you can't trust temporary workers: all of them belong to the same caste." Silently I thought, "Here are two Brahmin ladies grumbling about a lower-caste widow."

The same evening, they told me to contact Lataa Dai and inquire about her. Lataa dai used to help all the poor Nepali widows living in our neighborhood. Thus, he was familiar with the plight of Amir's mother. The following Saturday I went to my brother-in-law's clinic and met with Lataa Dai. When he saw me, he suddenly became somewhat agitated and said, "Oh, Babu, I forgot to tell you, Amir's mom asked me to thank you personally for taking Amir to the hospital and for being his guardian."

Irritated, I asked, "Why did she not come and thank me personally at my sister's home? And why has she not turned up for work? My sister has been cleaning the house and kitchen and pots and pans for so many days."

He looked at me, his almond-like eyes looking suddenly glassy, and said, "I am so sorry. I will find a new cleaning woman by this evening."

Still irritated, "I asked what happened to Amir's mom. Did she get a better paying job in Birla hospital?"

"No, she left; she went to Bhaksu Panjab," said Lataa Dai.

I was mystified. "Why?"

"Amir died a few days ago. After crying her heart out and fasting for days and nights, Amir's mom left the city. I accompanied her to the railway station and seated her in a Punjab mail train. Even in the railway station, she was crying and saying there is too much sorrow in this city."

I was numb with shock. And suddenly ashamed at my earlier irritation. The hurt and the helplessness I felt made a lasting imprint on my life. It pulsed through my veins like a slow poison during my entire stay in Kashi. I started asking Lataa Dai about the conditions of poor families and started visiting some of them with him.

The almost subhuman conditions I observed shocked me and had a tremendous impact on my heart and mind. I was, after all, a young, rural boy who had just come to the city and was just beginning to understand the harsh realities of urban life. I withdrew into myself, turning inward in introspection, and brooding over the question that kept repeating itself in my head, "Why? Why? Why? And what should I do?"

My sister noticed the change in me and asked, "What happened to you? Why are you so silent and glum all the time?"

She encouraged me to go out, to take a walk or go to the park. She was the only one with whom I could talk. In the house were her mother-in-law, over 75 years of age and waiting for *moksha*; and her husband, a homeopathic doctor always in search of patients, who were few and far between, causing a permanent financial crisis.

Amir's death had a lasting impact on my emotional evolution and intellectual growth. I began to wonder about the helpless condition of poor Nepali mothers and orphans living in the margins of a devout Hindu society. How could Amir die, I wondered, when he was almost back to full health? Why there was no medical help for Nepali sick children? Why did it take a Birla to provide care for us? Was it because we were in a foreign land and tolerated simply because we came from another Hindu country? We were second-class human beings: not quite refugees, yet living an existence of exile.

I decided to change my identity. A Bhattarai Brahmin boy from Nepal, I opted for the name Satish (a name of lord Shiva, the famous god of destruction) and Chandra as a middle name, for the college where I was going to be admitted. For my last name, I chose Prabasi, denoting someone in exile from their homeland. My chosen last name signified no caste. A few months after Amir's death, I was admitted to the ninth grade in Harish Chandra High School. When the headmaster asked my full name, I blurted out my new name rather confidently. He asked for my birth certificate or school certificate. I glanced at my brother-in-law, who had accompanied me.

He came to my rescue by saying, "Sir, as you well know, Nepal is a backward and illiterate country. We don't have a system of birth and death records, nor educational records. This young boy's father is a wise man, so he managed to obtain the services of a resident Indian teacher. I brought him to Kashi for further education. Since I know you and your college, I entrust him to your care and guidance."

The principal seemed well pleased. He asked me a few academic questions for which I had studied at home and, thus, was well prepared. After the preliminaries were over, no further questions were asked and I was admitted.

CHAPTER 5

MELANCHOLY DAYS

THERE was another consequence of Amir's death in my young life: at the age of 11, I was required to visit an Indian police station in the holy city of Kashi.

One evening, my brother-in-law entered my room; he appeared agitated and angry. He asked me in a stern voice if I had signed a hospital document as the guardian to Amir.

When I said yes, he flared up. "Why do you complicate your life and mess up mine? You know what happened today? For the first time in 30 years, two policemen entered my homeopathy clinic asking about you and the disappearance of Amir's mom. They asked several nonsensical questions. I did not even know you were a guardian to Amir. They asked me to inform you that you should report to the police station within three days."

"I am sorry I did not tell you. I thought it was small matter. An act of kindness."

"The police think you sold her to a famous brothel. I am sure you don't even know what brothel means." I was stunned. Perhaps the bewildered look on my face aroused compassion in him. He suggested I should find Laataa Dai and request him to accompany me to the police station the next day. The sooner the better.

I could not sleep that night, and early the next morning, I went out in search of Laata Dai. I found him at a tea stall where many of his colleagues, night guards and watchmen, used to hang out and gossip. I explained the whole story to Laataa Dai. He was suddenly alert, and his expression became grave.

"Babu, let's go immediately. This is a serious charge, and it can create further complications."

"But I have not taken my morning bath, Laataa Dai!"

"Forget it now," he said. "One should take a bath after visiting the police station, anyway. It may be a place for justice for others, but for Nepal's poor, it is a breeding ground for sin." He pulled my hand and we left the tea stall. Laataa Dai seemed to be quite familiar with the surroundings and even familiar with some constables. I understood this from his *salaam* greetings to them. I was intimidated by the officers' guns and the austere surroundings.

We were interviewed for more than an hour. Laataa Dai did most of the talking, giving as much detail about Amir's mom, the seven households where she worked part-time, and her last day in Kashi before her departure to Bhaksu. I still remember two of the questions asked of me.

"What will you think if we arrest you now for aiding a woman in a sinful profession?"

"What sinful profession? If you arrest me it will be an act of *adharma*." My Baba in Nepal used to say that all human acts can be classified in two ways: either in accord with *dharma*, or in accord with *adharma* (opposite of dharma).

The Head Constable smirked and asked, "What will be *adharma* here?"

I promptly replied, "Injustice. I helped a mother get treatment for her son. Why should I be arrested for this?"

Then he asked another question. "Do you know what Daal-Ki-Mandi is?"

I replied that in Nepal's Terai, "It is a wholesale market for lentils and grains."

There was a wave of laughter and joking in the police station. I was thoroughly confused and wondered what mistake I had committed now. After there was a little quiet, the chief inspector told me I was free to go.

"You are free from all our suspicions," he announced.

Relieved to be free of that frightening office, I ran out to the street. Little did I know, the Daal-Ki-Mandi was the largest red-light district in Banaras and that over 100 Nepali girls were working there as prostitutes. Laataa Dai explained that the police had suspected us of having sold Amir's mom to one of the gangs operating there. He also assured me not to worry and that he would explain everything to my sister and brother-in-law to their satisfaction.

Paradoxically, my brother-in-law and I grew distant, and our relationship became cold over time. Maybe he could not forget the fact that the police had entered his clinic because of my foolhardy action, or that I was too young for adult interaction but too grown up to be treated as a child. There was also an increasing economic burden on him as his family grew while income from his medical practice remained uncertain.

This created a mild tension at home that affected all of us. I grew aware of it over time, and my coping mechanism was to become increasingly introverted at home, fleeing the apartment every day for as long as I could.

When the weather was not too hot, I used to go to a local library. I was not yet a member there, so I just sat and read but could not borrow the books. I still remember the name of a popular local newspaper called *Aaj*. I remember it partly because it published my only Hindi poem, one I wrote in memory of Amir called "Prabasiyon ke Amir Sapane," "The Rich Dreams of the Exiled." Amir's name also meant "wealthy" or "rich" in Hindi and Urdu—the irony was not lost on me.

Often, I used to walk in the evening along the burning ghats of the Ganges, especially Manikarnika Ghat. It was a famous and fabled ghat where the rich and famous were brought for cremation. You could easily make out the rich: their pyres would be made of sandalwood soaked with pure ghee (clarified butter made from cows' milk) and adorned with layers and layers of rose garlands and other fragrant flowers. Then there were the bodies of the poor folk, unable to afford enough wood for a proper cremation, whose charred body parts and half-burnt bones would be visible upon a closer look. The acrid smell of these burning pyres would make me move away from the Manikarnika to other, quieter ghats, where boatmen with small dinghies would wait for visitors seeking a boat ride on the Ganges. During these evening outings, I developed a lifelong love for long walks and for bodies of water.

I remember Laataa Dai persuaded a buffalo-owning friend of his to teach me to swim "as the natives learnt it." So an 11-year-old lad from a land-locked country was pushed onto the tail end of a docile buffalo and told to firmly hold the tail. The fat and robust buffalo-owner followed us into the water lest I drown in the river.

After a few weeks of trial and error and gallons of holy water gulped down as I held onto the coarse, black tail of a buffalo, I learned to swim. I remember the day the buffalo owner said "Bacche [my boy], you have become a good swimmer. You will not drown in the Ganges." Lataa Dai, who always accompanied me, beamed at us in turn. I thanked them both and said that no matter how holy it was, I would not drink so much Ganges water again.

My brother-in-law was aware of my morning outings with Lataa Dai. He even encouraged them. But he was getting mystified and anxious about my long absences in the evenings. So he kept asking my sister, who in turn kept bothering me about it. One day, in the heat of irritation, I told my sister that I found my life quite miserable. There was nobody to talk to and nothing to talk about. There were only two solutions—I had already developed my fondness for numbered lists.

"Didi, could you ask your husband to get me a membership at the library, so I can borrow some books and read them at home?" Second, "I want to ask Baba to send me some money to buy a small electric Philips radio, which I will keep in my room, and I will promise my brother-in-law that I will not listen to Hindi film songs." She was taken aback by my requests. However, she agreed to both. Thus, my love—indeed, my passion—for books and radio (and later TV) began in Banaras.

CHAPTER 6

LIBRARY AND RADIO

I OBTAINED memberships to two libraries: the one in the neighborhood that was manned by a librarian named Shastri-ji, and a larger municipal library near my college that had many more books in English, Hindi, and several other Indian languages. These two institutions opened my mind and imagination to the worlds of the arts and literature.

The small Philips radio opened a window on the wider English-speaking world. At night, I would search for the frequencies for clear reception of the BBC, the Voice of America, and radio stations from distant places that I was not even aware existed. Thus, the world of my imagination and the news of the physical world helped me to overcome my acute feelings of ennui and loneliness.

I studied for four years in Banaras. The first two years led to the completion of my high-school education. As I mentioned earlier, I was a "home student" in the sense that I was tutored by Master Sahib in my home. I therefore needed a certifiable proof of high-school education. The first two years of schooling in India helped me obtain it. This led to an additional two years of university-level study at Banaras Hindu University. The degree was called an I.A., intermediate in arts. In those days, the education system in India was based on three layers of learning and academic examination: high school; intermediate-level study for two years, followed by another two years' study to obtain a bachelor of arts; and, finally, higher education, leading to a master's degree.

I was fortunate, in retrospect, to have studied in India in the early days of its independence. It was a five-year-young republic brimming with boundless optimism. Unshackled from the British, yet burdened by millions of refugees fortunate enough to survive the bloodbath of partition. Proud of the nonviolent philosophy of Mahatma Gandhi, India was trying to weave a distinct identity from contrary and conflicting strands of culture and ideology.

A parliamentary democracy led by the regal, charming Jawaharlal "Pandit" Nehru, India was fatally attracted to the Soviet model of development. A secular country according to its written constitution, India was buffeted by Hindu passions and deeply held traditions of caste and creed. Consequently, India's vision of socialist pattern of development was often in conflict with the capitalistic mode of enterprises already existing in abundance in India.

It was an exhilarating time for higher education in Banaras, and I was influenced by competing strata of emerging Indian society. This was reflected in four notable personalities I had the good fortune to meet and befriend. The first was Shastri-ji, the librarian. Shastri-ji had a multifaceted personality. A devotee of Lord Shiva with a rather large vibhuti of white ash on his forehead (tika), he was an extrovert with a quick smile and a helpful attitude for all. He had a master's degree in English literature and a Shastri degree (Master's Degree in Sanskrit) in Sanskrit studies. He was equally eloquent in Sanskrit, Hindi, English, and his mother tongue, Marathi. During our four years of friendship, he made me aware of and developed my sensibility to Sanskrit literature and philosophy. He dwelt at length on the similarities between the Vedanta and British author Aldous Huxley's *The Perennial Philosophy*. He was a tolerant Hindu but a fierce nationalist. Even now, I am struck by a statement he made often: "Our prime minister is an Englishman at heart, who is called Pandit. He wears a white Indian cap with the blessings of Great Mahatma [Gandhi]." His skill in debating and his facility with language inspired me to take part in high school and college debates.

The second was Professor Dutta, my teacher of history. He was a specialist in European thought and the Renaissance, a dour-faced introvert with wavy Bengali hair and huge black glasses. A refugee from Dhaka, recently carved out as the capital of East Pakistan, he had a humane yet cynical view of history.

There was Professor K. K. Shah, a strikingly handsome, tall Kashmiri who was Sufi by faith and well-versed in Persian and English literature. He was our English professor, jolly by nature and always helpful to students. He was especially kind to me because I was proficient in English.

The fourth person was someone who I called Mysterious Dada, to whom I was introduced by a college friend. He was a tall Bengali with shoulder-length black hair and large, luminous eyes, and he was totally committed to the Communist cause and its ideology. He used to run a pavement-based bookstall in front of a movie theater in a busy thoroughfare called Godauliya. Dada introduced me to Russian writers. After we became friends and he trusted me, he would say, "They are treasures of humanity in Soviet jackets." Thus, I was introduced to the world of Pushkin, Turgenev, Dostoevsky, and Maxim Gorky along with Marx and Mao.

Professor Shah was keen that I should continue my studies in English literature in Banaras. He even arranged a scholarship for me. I was inclined to go back to Kathmandu for my graduate studies. Historical events propelled me to this decision. The century-long repressive Rana regime had crumbled on the initiative of King Tribhuvan, who was deftly assisted by the newly independent India. It was alleged in Banaras's Nepali political community that King Tribhuvan was encouraged to flee his palace, Narayanhiti Durbar, and take shelter in New Delhi. The Indian ambassador to Nepal was believed to be crafty by nature and good at political machinations. He invited His Majesty the King to visit the temple of Shiva in Kathmandu, Pashupathinath. On the king's return journey, the royal party's two cars were diverted to the Indian mission and granted political asylum. Rumor had it that the Indian army sent a plane to fly the royal family to New Delhi. The second prince, Gyanendra, was left in the palace to convince the Rana prime minister that the king had no intention of leaving the country. After Mohan Shamsher—the Rana prime minister at the time—learned from his spies that the king had been taken by Indian diplomats, he was furious and made plans to install the child Gyanendra as the new king. The prime minister even arranged to mint silver coins with Gyanendra's portrait so that the average Nepali would believe that there had been a peaceful royal transition.

These rumors and the political developments in the Indo-Nepal relationship gave students and political leaders in Banaras daily fuel for rumor-mongering and analysis. I was privy to these discussions through my family connection with a man named Bal Chandra Sharma, who was the stepbrother of my brother-in-law. I remember that his famous book on Nepal's history, called *Nepalko Itihaas ko Rup-Rekha*, or *A Historical Outline of Nepal*, was in the process of being printed in Banaras. It had to be retrieved from the press in order to amend and adapt the last few chapters of the book, and I was given the task of courier to bring the old drafts from the press and carry the new versions back to the press.

In these politically active circles, there were a couple of people whom I distinctly remember. One was the legendary and still-revered national poet of Nepal, Laxmi Prasad Devkota. My memory of the poet consists of his bright forehead, his chain-smoking habit, and his talent for churning out memorable poems anywhere at the request of a friend. The second person was Narayan Banskota, who was at that time the editor of a Nepali-language progressive quarterly called *Pragati* ("*Progress*"). I still remember that Devkota composed more than a dozen poems for his editor friend Banskota. On several occasions, Banskota would ask Laxmi-ji to compose a couple of poems with a plea, "My magazine does not have enough content. I still need to fill up some pages; Laxmi-ji, can you do a free verse, one folk poem, and whatever else strikes your fancy? But I need it in two days." The poet would reply with a twinkle in his eyes, "Please give me a pack or two of Capstan cigarettes," a popular brand among the educated and the elite. Nowadays, I wonder with a sense of awe and astonishment at the contribution of those cigarettes to Nepali poetry.

These friendships and meetings had given rise to curiosity in my mind about Nepal in general and Kathmandu in particular. I had never been to Kathmandu before, but I had heard so much about its natural beauty, as contrasted against its lack of hygiene and its horrible social conditions. I had trouble reconciling these two pictures in my imagination.

Mr. Banskota had fired up my imagination about the contradictory situation in Nepal by quoting certain passages from books by notable European historians who had visited the country in the eighteenth and nineteenth centuries.

One passage that stuck in my memory was from Charles-Marie Gustave le Bon's 1886 book *Voyage to Nepal*, in which he claims, "I doubt that an opium eater has dreamt, in his wildest dreams, of a more fantastic architecture than the one in this strange city." He was referring to the temples and palaces, Newari mandala-form buildings, in Patan and Bhaktapur in the Kathmandu valley.

I contrasted that with a passage from another book called *History of Nepal* written by a famous Sanskrit scholar from France, Sylvain Levi. He wrote that the "entire population of the city was absolutely, totally, radically, ignorant." Further, wherever he went, he was thronged by gormless and foul-smelling crowds. "Justice must be given to the Newars, I have seen some of them wash themselves at least once in their lives."

These contradictory views and images of Nepal led me to believe that I must go and resume my college education there. I wanted to go back to my home country, albeit to a city I had never seen.

Some of the political personalities I had met in Banaras had reached Kathmandu, according to news reports, and efforts at shaping the democratic Nepal were underway. It excited many students like me.

My mind was made up by another piece of news I heard over my little Philips radio. One morning, the BBC World news announced that the king of Nepal had died in Switzerland. The reception was quite faint, but I could make out that his personal Swiss nurse had read out the statement. I surfed various radio stations until, at long last, the English-language broadcast of All India Radio confirmed the news of the king's death. It was the year 1955, and I was fifteen years old. The next day, I told my sister and brother-in-law that I planned to leave for Nepal within a month. My sister was more perplexed than my brother-in-law. But I remember that Professor Shah was shocked the most, and he tried to dissuade me by saying, "Satish, you don't realize it, but you are making the biggest mistake of your life."

CHAPTER 7

EXIT FROM BANARAS

I NEEDED four weeks to travel from Banaras to Kathmandu. My father and I decided to meet at the last railhead before entering Nepal, at a place called Raxaul. Baba had arranged for me to stay with relatives in Kathmandu. This made my arrival in Kathmandu, the capital city of Nepal, smooth and comfortable.

Long before I boarded the train to Raxaul, I began to feel all kinds of excitement and anxiety. There was the excitement of meeting my father again after four years. I was acutely conscious of the significance of living in Kathmandu, a city I had never seen even though it was my country's capital city. I had read that some years ago a few British cars had been dismantled at the checkpoint at Bhimphedi and 28 porters would carry them into the valley to be reassembled in Kathmandu under the supervision of a Scottish engineer. My brother-in-law told me, "Since there are no roads in the valleys and mountains, you may have to walk a couple of days before you reach Kathmandu. You should carry very few things from Banaras—maybe not even your Philips radio, as there is no electric power for common people." Only the ruling Ranas and palace people had access to electricity.

Following his advice, I carried a dozen books, including a history book by Percival London, *A Historical Outline of Nepal* by Bal Chandra Sharma, books by British poets Byron, Shelley, and Keats, and a political book called *How to Be a Good Communist* by Liu Shaoqi.

During my four years in Banaras, I had read Jawaharlal Nehru's acclaimed book, *The Discovery of India*. At the beginning of my journey to Kathmandu, I had hoped to discover the real Nepal. The Nepal of Laataa Dai, Amir ki Ama, the poor and downtrodden, the children of various ethnic groups with different capacities —*Santaan thari- thari ka,* as the Nepali poet M.B. B. Shah wrote. I therefore decided I wanted to study sociology and economics in Nepal.

After a few weeks of roaming around and taking in the sights, sound, and aromas of the city, I began to explore my chances for admission to the only college in the country, Tri-Chandra College, for a bachelor of arts. It was established in 1918 by the Rana prime minister Chandra Shamsher. It is claimed that he was the most astute and intelligent prime minister, and with his combination of wisdom and craftiness, he ruled the country for almost 30 years.

His brothers and close relatives were against the establishment of the college, arguing that, "It will pollute the mind of our subjects and destroy our system of administration." The prime minister overruled them, countering, "Unless we train a cadre of loyal and educated bureaucrats, the strong winds of political change and transformation already sweeping through the neighboring [Indian] states, such as Bengal and Bihar, will undermine our rule."

Given the specific goal of political control through higher education, the college's administration would meet three criteria: the curriculum would be approved by the government; each potential student would be interviewed and assessed as to his or her loyalty by the director of education, who would always be appointed from the Rana clan; and finally, the principal of the college would be interviewed intensively by the education director prior to his appointment.

Coming from Banaras, I did not know the purpose behind the establishment of the college, but with the new political changes in Nepal, the rules and regulations regarding admission had changed. However, there were still remnants of the past in the college.

For example, the three subjects I wished to pursue—economics, politics, and sociology—were not offered by the college. When I was interviewed by the principal, he gave me a keen and withering look and told me to study in India; these new subjects were not approved for teaching by the college.

I was shattered and deeply dejected. Silently, I blamed myself, thinking that my risky decision to come to Kathmandu had ruined my future. I remembered K. K. Shah's prophetic warning against studying in Nepal. His last letter, which I received in Kathmandu, indicated that he had arranged for my admission to Banaras Hindu University in two departments: English literature and modern history. He had also said in the letter, "Your placement cannot be reserved beyond three months; therefore, let me know soonest." After the debacle at Tri-Chandra college, I was too ashamed and embarrassed to reply to Professor Shah. I had lost a poetry-loving friend—a loss I regret to this day.

There was no point to staying in Kathmandu any longer, so I made arrangements to return to Govindpur. I packed up my rickety metal suitcase, a carry-bag full of books and some sacred offerings. These came from Pashupathinath, a temple of Shiva, and from the temple of Dakshin-Kali, a kind yet ferocious mother goddess greatly revered in Nepal. I also bid goodbye to Damodar *kaka* and went to see Subhadra *sanima* (familial expressions for uncle and aunt).

I told my aunt I was going back to my village in a week or two, so this would be my last visit to convey my regards and to request that she come to Govindpur as she had in the past. She was somewhat baffled, and her expression changed. She said, "Why don't you stay on?" and I retorted, "To do what, Sanima?"

My aunt Subhadra Devi was an extraordinary person with a strong personality for a woman of those times. Married at an early age, she lived in Banaras and gave birth to a baby boy. The happiness of the family was shattered when her husband suddenly died, probably from a heart attack. Nobody was sure of the cause of death because there were no adequate medical facilities to examine him. The young widow was confronted with unimaginable disaster—the challenge of raising an infant and earning money to sustain her family. After learning of the hardships suffered by Subhadra sanima, Baba invited her to stay in our home in Govindpur. Consequently, Subhadra and her bright young son Ramu came and lived with us for many years.

Later, she moved back to Banaras to help with her son's education, and after he completed high school, Subhadra shifted her family to Kathmandu and found a job in the house of a man named General Thapa. Thapa helped Ramu gain admission to Tri-Chandra College and facilitated the award of a modest scholarship.

Subhadra Devi was extraordinarily perceptive of the value of higher education. Therefore, she did not oppose her son's decision, in later years, to study in Calcutta.

My aunt's house had a modest yard and a small orchard with various species of subtropical fruit trees. I had never seen grapefruit or daarim (a subclass of pomegranate) trees before moving to her house, so the orchard looked exotic to eyes accustomed to the trees and plants in the flatlands of the Terai and northern India.

At one point during my courtesy call, Sanima and I both fell silent, lost in thought. After a few minutes, she told me that she would come to see me in my rented room in two days' time. "I will send some gifts for your family, so don't go loitering around on that day." She did come two days later with a porter. Jokingly, I said, "Is he the gift you are sending?" She smiled with a twinkle in her eyes. "Instead of returning to Govindpur, you are coming to my house in Naxal (a neighborhood in Kathmandu). I brought this porter to help carry your things. So please load them up and follow me. I have a big room in which a friend of my son is living. It is a big room, so it has enough space to put your bed. The only rule I will insist on is that you must close the main gate by nine p.m. every evening." Delighted, I followed the porter and her.

Nepal did not have then, nor does it now, a system of social security or economic support for broken, helpless families. Mutual support from kith and kin was the only means to overcome a family tragedy. It was this tradition of helping each other that paved the way, I believe, for my continued stay, and future study, in Kathmandu.

CHAPTER 8

KATHMANDU

T HUS began another adventure! Sanima reintroduced me to her son, whom I had not met since childhood. I now called him Devendra-daaju, and her daughter-in-law, Sarala-bhauju. In Nepal, one's elders and respected relatives are always called by an honorific. *Daaju* literally translates as elder brother, but is used more generally; *bhauju* is the title given to sisters-in-law. In the dimly lit dining room, I also met Sarva Dev Verma, another guest in their household who became my lifelong friend. He used to call my aunt 'Aama', another honorific term to express respect for an elderly lady of the house.

My first evening in Sanima's household was memorable. Her son, Devendra Raj Upadhyaya, whom I knew in my village Govindpur as Ramu, recently had been appointed as the Director of Radio Nepal. For several years, he had worked in New Delhi, India, as the chief of the Gorkhali Service of All India Radio. After King Tribhuvan returned to Nepal and established a liberal government, some of the previously exiled leaders of the political party Nepali Congress took positions in the new government. Devendra Upadhyaya was offered the job of the director of radio services.

Over time, I came to know the strengths and vulnerabilities of each member of the household. Devendra-daaju, now the head of his family, was completely devoted and obedient to his widowed mother, who had sacrificed so much to educate him and promote his career. Affectionately, he used to call his own mother *Didi*, elder sister. He was brilliant, sarcastic, and self-absorbed in some respects. Yet he could also be generous, warm, and kind, depending on his mood.

Sarala-bhauju was regal and beautiful. She was introverted and didn't talk much, being a young bride and new to the family. Some people mistook her shyness for pride or arrogance, though she had neither. Over time, I would come to know how thoughtful, kind, and generous her true nature was.

There was also a housemaid and helper living with the family who was called Gopal ki Aama. She was very helpful and always alert to the needs of other members of the household. From the very first day of my stay with my Sanima, she reminded me of Amir ki Aama, who had had such an impact on me during my days in Banaras.

During my first year at their home, I didn't understand the tensions I sensed between Sanima, Devendra-daaju, and Sarala-bhauju. As a newcomer living in their family and the youngest member of the household, I was not expected to understand the family's dynamics or the background of their interactions. However, Sarva Dev Verma, who was equally friendly with all three, helped me understand the situation.

One Saturday morning a terrible accident occurred. Saturday is normally a day of rest and holiday in Nepal. Devendra-daaju and his wife Sarala-bhauju had gone on a picnic with his young son Sachindra and their family friends. They drove on the newly constructed mountainous route called Tika Bhairav road. Their jeep plunged almost fifty meters below the road. Young Sachindra died on the spot. Sarala-bhauju was gravely injured and lost a kidney. Miraculously, Devendra-daaju was physically unscathed, though the loss of his first son shattered him to his core. Sarala-bhauju was rushed to the ICU at a hospital run by the American Christian Fathers. The head of the hospital was a doctor called Father Moran.

When I returned to Sanima's in the evening with Sarva Dev Verma, the place was dark and silent. I asked Gopal-ki-Aama the reason for the silence and darkness; she wept incoherently as she narrated the scale of the tragedy.

We were stunned, at a loss as to what we should do. The hospital, Shanta Bhavan, was in the town of Patan, and there was no public transport to get us there. Taxi services were nonexistent in Kathmandu in 1956, and the telephone was a privilege of the few—royalty and high government officials. Verma-ji and I, therefore, decided to wait in our room. The next morning, a disheveled Devendra-daaju came home and informed us that one of us had to spend the night in the hospital to look after Sarala-bhauju, who was still unconscious. I offered to go immediately because Verma-ji had to work. Sarala-bhauju gradually recovered.

The first few months of my stay in Naxal were a period of rest and recreation in the mild and invigorating weather of Kathmandu. My friendship with Mr. Verma deepened. He was a senior civil servant in the Central Secretariat of the government, with the designated title of Registrar of Co-operative Department. It was a part of the Ministry of Agriculture. His letters of recommendation helped me get my membership to the British Library and the American Cultural Center. I was enormously grateful to Mr. Verma for recommending my membership to these institutions. My attraction to these libraries was for the books and journals. The libraries also had the most hygienic and cleanest bathrooms in the valley. Suffice it to say that my physical and intellectual health both improved considerably thanks to the libraries.

In my lonely and uncertain days in Kathmandu, Verma-ji's

company was a source of solace and mental relaxation. A man of slight build and a simpatico face, kind and friendly by nature, he had the great gift of making friends with people of all ages. His office hours were 10:00 am to 5:00 pm, after which he would walk to New Road to meet with his friends or visit taverns around Kathmandu. He suggested I join him on his walks around New Road. As I used to spend my afternoons in the reading room of the American Library, also on New Road, it was easy for me to meet him there. Late in the evening, we would walk back home, swaying on the rough roads. I vividly recall those walks, when I would press the cell-operated torch for light on the road and Verma-ji would sing in his melodious voice a few couplets of a Nepali love song: "*Aye Patali dekhe pachi maya lagcha na dekhekai jaati!*" "*Oh, slim one, when I see you, I fall in love; it is better not to behold you!*"

I would lock the main gate after reaching home, then Verma-ji and I would tiptoe to the wooden staircase, pausing for a minute or two to ensure that Sanima was not awake. We would take off our shoes lest they make noise on the creaky stairs and quickly make our way to our room. Relieved that we were not noticed by anyone in our inebriated condition, we would change our clothes and enter the kitchen for our evening meal.

After dinner we would return to our room, close the door, open the small window, and enjoy the nightcap on which Verma-ji insisted.

The ritual of nightcaps led to one somewhat unsavory event. One morning Sanima, with an angry face and blazing eyes, entered our room and accused Verma-ji, "Have you no shame? You drink in the room, which I reluctantly tolerate, and now you have started throwing the drinks' bottles near the outhouse in the garden! People will bleed if they step on the pieces of glass!"

Bewildered, Verma-ji denied the accusations. "Ama, I have never thrown these bottles in your garden. Being afraid that you will see them, I collect them in a jute bag and throw them away on my way to Singha Durbar."

Sanima warned, "If I see another empty bottle again in my garden it will be the last day of your stay in my house, Sarv Dev."

After she left, I secured the door of our room and apologized, saying, "You have been scolded for my actions. On some cold wintry nights, I thought it would be convenient to throw them from the window of the room to a corner of the garden where Sanima does not go. As our ill luck would have it, Sanima went this morning to pick some ripe persimmon fruit in the orchard."

Verma-ji stared at me and said, "Don't say our bad luck; it's only my bad luck, not yours. I will never be able to drink in this room again."

I told him not to worry. "I will take the assignment of disposing of the bottles in the morning when I go out to walk or to the library." I placated him, and the pleasure of our nightcaps continued until both of us moved to Chitwan district.

One evening, as we walked back from New Road, I asked Verma-ji about the love lyric he often sang. "Is there is a story behind it?"

He narrated his sad love story.

During his Colombo Plan–sponsored journey to Ceylon, Verma-ji fell in love with a nurse named Shirley. She was madly in love with Verma-ji and wanted to marry him and raise a family in Colombo. But Verma-ji was not prepared to live in Ceylon, so after six months of being madly in love, Verma-ji came back to Nepal. Shirley wrote him letters for a couple of years. When we returned home, Verma-ji showed me some of her letters, which he still cherished. After couple of drinks, he would remember his svelte girlfriend and sing the same melancholy song, "*Dekhe pachi maya lagcha .... Na dekhekai jaati!// When I see you I fall in love, better not to behold you!*"

The first year of my stay in Kathmandu was painful and disturbing on many levels. After the initial euphoria of having arrived in the capital city, my excitement began to wear thin. I could not study the three subjects I wanted for my graduate work, economics, politics, and sociology (EPS), which I intended to pursue. There was no national university in Nepal, and the two colleges in the valley were affiliated with Patna University, which was viewed as a second-rate institution by most academics in India and Nepal. Often, I regretted that I had foregone studying at Banaras Hindu University.

I joined the National Night College, which was a private endeavor initiated by professor Shanker Dev Pant. Today, the college is named in his honor and his bust has been installed in the campus. The principal of the college was candid enough to tell me, "We do not have courses on sociology. If you insist on studying these courses, you must do it on your own. Consequently, if you fail the exams, it will be your responsibility." I took on his challenge.

I had time on my hands during the day and was extremely busy in the evenings. My reading habits developed in Banaras helped me a great deal. I frequented the American Library on New Road, and the British Council Library on Durbar Marg during the daytime. Thanks to the habits instilled in me by Professors Shah and Dutta in Banaras, I was able to broaden my mental horizons.

After approximately six months, I saw an ad in the national newspaper, *Gorkhapatra*, announcing the establishment of the Teachers Training College, funded by USAID. The classes would run from nine in the morning to three in the afternoon. The selected students were offered a handsome scholarship—400 rupees a month! —which was more than double the salary of first-level government officials. A section officer in Nepal earned 175 rupees per month in those days. Even this sum was supposed to be a blessing for maintaining a family in Kathmandu.

I was excited by the prospect of spending my days at the college while simultaneously earning a handsome amount. I began to focus on books on American education, borrowing several from the American Library. There were 175 candidates who appeared for the entrance exam. I think many of them were attracted by the 400 rupees rather than the prospect of being a trained teacher; I was one of them.

It was my first exposure to the American system of exams and educational methodology. The exam paper had multiple-choice questions, pointed true-or-false questions, and brief essays. It was to be capped by an oral exam to evaluate one's command of the English language. I distinctly remember the names and faces of the three examiners who interviewed me in the afternoon: Professor Wood, a professor of education sent by the US government; Professor Basnet, a liquor-loving professor of English literature; and Professor Upreti, the principal-designate of the college appointed by the government of Nepal.

I thought I had done well in the exam. It was a novel experience for all the students interested in admission to the new college. In keeping with the American system of education, we were given questions stretched over a dozen pages. Some questions were multiple choice, some were just 'yes/no,' some related to history, and at the end, there was an open-ended essay. I remember it vividly because it was so different from the British/Indian type of exam with which we were familiar. Thanks to my membership of the American Library and my reading of American curricula I was better prepared for the examination. After two weeks, I received a letter from the college authority asking me to appear for another interview. I was nonplussed because I had thought I had done well, and no one else was invited for another interview. If I had failed, I reasoned, there was no need to call me in. Yet if I did pass, why another interview? This worrisome question was answered when my guardian, Mr. Upadhyaya, congratulated me, saying that I had done extremely well—so much so that the examiners suspected the question paper was leaked in advance. Professor Narendra Basnet, whom Devendra Daju knew well, inquired about me and my reading habits.

I was both happy and annoyed by this piece of information. Nonetheless, I reappeared for the oral interview, and it turned out to be rather memorable. The panel of three professors asked me some pointed—and some silly—questions.

Their opening salvo was, "How did you obtain the question

paper in advance?" In anger, I jokingly replied that Professor Wood had passed it to me so I could be better aware of American-style questions. Wood, who was right in front of me, guffawed.

On a serious note, I said, "I have been preparing for this exam for six hours a day, reading all kinds of books and materials at the American Library."

Their second question was, "How many monarchies are in Asia in addition to Nepal?"

I arrogantly asked, "Should I start from East Asia or West Asia?" to which Professor Basnet said, "Start from the West."

I listed them all, going from Jordan, the westernmost monarchy in Asia, all the way to Japan, the easternmost. I had the grace to acknowledge Professor Dutta, the refugee historian from Bangladesh, who had taught me in Banaras.

After several other questions, ranging from Bhanu-Bhakta, the first Nepali poet, to Shakespeare, the oral exam lasted for a long hour. The members of the panel shook my hand and said, "Our suspicion was misplaced. You have secured first position in the exam."

I achieved weeklong fame in Nepali academic circles, inspiring two questions: "Who is this Prabasi, and how did he get this score?"

CHAPTER 9

TROUBLE AGAIN

IT was eye-opening for me to experience the equality between teachers and students that American professors encouraged. The emphasis upon questioning, rather than learning by rote, the professors' encouragement to use the library as a resource, and our weekly or fortnightly exams exposed me to another facet of American education, so different from the Indo-British system that I was used to. .

My appreciation for the US system of education and the holistic development of my personality made me a more polished young man.

In Nepali, they say that good things don't last long. My second year at the college brought unforeseen disaster upon many of my friends and me. A rumor started floating around the college that some of the bureaucrats in the Ministry of Education had made a move to reduce our US government scholarship to equal the pay of the civil service's section officers. There were complaints that young boys should not be receiving more than 175 rupees per month. The generosity of the US grant was embarrassing and demoralizing to some of the civil servants in Singh Durbar. It was further alleged that a recommendation had already been sent to the chief secretary of Nepal's government to reduce the scholarship amount; the surplus funds would go to the Department of Education to hire more teachers. It was a clever argument that few could dispute in a society with widespread illiteracy like Nepal. But the sudden realization that our stipend was going to be reduced to match the pay for Nepali civil servants made us furious. What really hurt us was the facile comparison of our scholarship with the minimum salary of section officer working for the government.

We decided that a group of three students would meet the education minister and the administrators of the college to find out the truth and, if possible, stop the reduction to our stipends. The meeting with the education minister turned out to be a total disaster; he gave us a speech and said, "The US government will not be paying you throughout your life. After graduation, when you join the labor market, you will have to get used to our national norms of payment. So don't feel privileged." Our meeting with Professor Wood, the education advisor to the college, exposed the helplessness of a donor in guiding a willful and obstinate recipient—in this case, the Ministry of Education. He was sympathetic but told us, "Look, boys, as much as I sympathize with you guys, we cannot do anything against the judgment of His Majesty's Government."

This left the student body in a dilemma as to what our next steps should be. Brash and young as we were, we decided to hold a sit-in protest – *a dharana*. We organized a meeting of all the students. I distinctly remember, even now, the sunlit grounds of Chet Bhavan, the palace building where the college was housed in those days. I was given the task of summarizing what happened so far and set the agenda for our discussion. There were various opinions among the students — some wanted to talk with the Prime Minister, going over the head of the Education Minister.

Others believed we should give ground. A vocal half-dozen of us thought we should not take this lying down. Given my fluency in English, they decided I should be the leader of the protest group and continue our resistance. After a week's consultation and strategy sessions we thought we should learn from the protest movements in India and go all out against the government's decision to reduce our stipends.

First, we boycotted classes. We realized after a week or so that our passive resistance wasn't getting any results. A more radical strategy was needed. One of us suggested that we should buy a *bhote talcha*, a big and sturdy padlock used in Nepal's prisons, and surprise Mr. Wood the following Monday when he came to his office.

On that fateful morning, five of us pretended to seek an appointment with Mr. Wood in his office. We all entered his room as if we needed some urgent assistance. The gentle professor was intrigued: his first question was, "What is it now?" Four of us left the room while I kept him engaged in conversation. There was clapping from outside, a signal to me that I should run out of the room. I made an excuse to leave, and we locked the office from outside.

We were pleased with our accomplishment. Some of the students brought us grapefruit, a typical Nepali snack in the winter months. We sat on the college grounds and enjoyed the fruits of our labor. Within three hours of our mischief, a Nepali police van containing a dozen or so policemen entered the college grounds. The police were shouting, "Who are the culprits?" When they saw the five of us on the sunlit grounds, they pounced upon us and hauled us into their van. We learned later that a senior professor at the college had called both the Ministry of Education and the office of the United States Operation Mission (USOM, the forerunner to USAID in Nepal) informing them of a major incident unheard of in the Kathmandu valley.

We were taken to the police station in the nearby district of Lalitpur and detained there overnight. Even the police were innocent in those days in Nepal. They kept all of us in one room, which gave us ample opportunity to further refine our strategy together. We were shocked and afraid, but we needed a way to get out of this situation. After a long discussion among ourselves, we decided that all five of us would leave the college. That may have been the only way to avoid suspension. A friend of ours had a relative working at the *Gorkhapatra*. He promised that after we were released, he would ensure that the news of our quitting would make it into the paper.

The next morning, the superintendent of the Lalitpur District Police spoke to us for half an hour and asked us to sign a statement promising that we would not indulge in such anti-national activities as locking up a foreign guest again. We were thoroughly shaken by that time, so we agreed immediately.

That was not the end of my troubles, though. The minister of education had somehow found out that I was the ringleader and spokesperson of the group. He sent a letter to my guardian, Mr. Upadhyaya, demanding that I meet him within three days or be dismissed from the college. Mr. Upadhyaya, himself a senior government employee, was shocked and gave me another verbal dressing down. I went to see the minister, not knowing what else I could do. He gave me three conditions: disappear from the valley immediately; never again think of doing a graduate course in teacher training; and do not associate with the remaining students at the college for the next two years, lest similar unruly behavior happen there again. In response, I said that I could meet the last two conditions, but as to the first, I had nowhere else to go. Instead I proposed that I could spend my days at home and resume the night-college studies that I had been pursuing prior to joining the College of Education.

I guess the minister was pleased with my quick acceptance of two of the conditions; he agreed to my request to stay in Kathmandu but not associate with my former colleagues.

I was relieved and extremely worried after narrowly avoiding my expulsion from Kathmandu. Future courses of action for me were career-limiting. The little savings I had made from my scholarship would be enough, I thought, for an additional couple of months' stay in Kathmandu, because I did not have to pay for rent and food. Should I go back to Govindpur, my ancestral village, or hang around here in search of a low-paying job?

I shared my dilemma with Verma-ji, my cheerful friend, who insisted that I stay in the city. My immediate worry was how to break the news of my expulsion to Subhadra sanima. My observant aunt would notice if I started staying home in the mornings. I therefore decided to leave my room at my usual hour and go to the American Library or the British Library and come home at my usual hour as though nothing had changed.

CHAPTER 10

A FLICKER OF LIGHT

I ENTERED an uncertain period in my life after I was forced to give up my studies. I spent hours at the local libraries and hours with friends, especially Sarva Dev Verma, and we became close friends. A flicker of light appeared when Subhadra sanima came to my room one morning and said, "Babu, you have met Sharada. She is a studious girl, but unfortunately, for the last two years she failed in her English test. She cannot be admitted to college for a bachelor's degree unless she passes that test. Could you please give her a tutorial in English for an hour or so after you come back from college? She will pay you a tuition fee." I readily agreed to tutor her but declined the offer of payment.

During one of our tutorial sessions, Sharada told me her brother Dhruva worked in the commissary of USOM. She said that her brother had heard a rumor that the mission was looking for an articulate translator for a senior black officer stationed at its Rapti Valley Multipurpose Development Project. Her brother would recommend me for an interview if I was interested in the job. I was confused: until then I had neither heard of the Rapti Valley project nor about various types of grants provided by the USOM to different ministries of Nepal.

I told her that I would consult Verma-ji in the evening and convey the message to Dhruv-ji. Excited and almost feverish, I sought Verma-ji's advice during our nightcap session.

His face brightened, and he strongly suggested that I go for the interview. He urged that I try my best to get the job because it would give both of us a chance to work together in the Rapti Valley.

The next day, I told Sharada that I was interested in the job and that her brother should suggest my name for an interview. Within a week, I was called for an interview in Rabi Bhavan, and thus my life journey took another sharp turn: from Chet Bhavan, the location of my College of Education to Rabi Bhavan, the sprawling palace where USOM was located.

A few weeks after my interview, I received a letter from USOM informing me that I had been selected for the job. I had given the interviewers my friend Mr. Verma's office address for contacting me because there were no house addresses in Kathmandu those days. Also, there were no telephones and the postman was extremely unreliable. It turned out that my decision to give Mr. Verma's address had another advantage: since he was going to work for the Rapti Valley project on a short assignment for the Government of Nepal, I synchronized my departure with his date of departure. In the first week of August in 1957, at the age of seventeen, I left for Chitwan with Sarva Dev Verma in a Jeep station wagon, issued to us courtesy of USOM.

July and August are terrible months to travel in Nepal. It is the monsoon season, a time of incessant rain and mudslides in the hills, and the sudden swelling of mountain rivers often causes death and disasters all over the country. The monsoon rains continue for three to four months, starting the first week of July and lasting until the end of September or early October. We reached Bharatpur, the headquarters of the Rapti Valley project, after two difficult days of travel with unforeseen delays caused by sudden floods.

The Rapti Valley project was the first of its kind in Nepal. It had elements of land development, including the resettlement of thousands of farmers displaced from their homes by floods in western Nepal, especially in the districts of Lamjung, Kaski, and Nuwakot. The ferocity of the floods had forced even well-to-do farmers into the forest areas of Chitwan district. Hundreds of them died in the western part of the district, sleeping under the trees and succumbing to malaria.

During this period, some of the senior bureaucrats visited the king, Mahendra. They requested that a plan for the resettlement of those people be prepared and financed. The king's first two queries were whether there was enough land there, and who would give us the resources and funds for the project.

Incidentally, a newly graduated agriculturist had also approached the palace with a proposal for the resettlement of the flood-afflicted farmers. His name was Krishna Bom Malla, and he was from the western district of Kaski. This district is known for beautiful lakes and is the starting point for treks to the Annapurna massif.

Mr. Malla was an extraordinary person. Over six feet tall, with an imposing personality, he was introverted by nature but quite happy to interact with small groups of strangers. He had recently graduated from the agricultural university in Naini, near Allahabad in India.

Unknown to the government bureaucrats, Mr. Malla's proposal to the king suggested that a large swath of grassland between the eastern part of Chitwan and the western part of the district could be used for the resettlement of the flood-affected hill people.

After I started working in Chitwan, Malla shared the origin of the Rapti Valley project and explained his appointment as the director. Malla said that His Majesty the King had ordered him to come to Narayanhiti Palace. During his audience, the king asked Malla several pertinent questions: "Given the chance, how will you begin this project? What kind of minimum resources will you need?" "From where will we get funding or finances for it?" "What kind of manpower or staff would be required?"

Cutting to the chase, Malla said that he would need two elephants to traverse the grassland, a pair of sturdy surveyors, and most importantly, His Majesty's permission to initiate discussion with USOM about seeking joint funding for the project.

It seems the king was highly impressed by Mr. Malla's approach and agreed to all three requests.

My first impression of Bharatpur was bewildering. It was a sultry, humid place surrounded by an unending canopy of tall hardwood trees called *Sal*. The unbearable heat and consequent unending streams of sweat forced most people to work bare-chested with minimal clothing.

I vividly remember Verma-ji's instruction to our local cook that each evening he should place four kerosene lanterns around our thatched hut. When I asked Verma-ji about the reason for this, he replied, "Wild animals, especially tigers, roam around this area during the night. The lanterns keep them from entering the hut."

Chitwan is an unusual district. In the foothills of the mighty Himalayas, this densely forested, hot and humid place teeming with wildlife has three distinct features. The eastern part of Chitwan is crisscrossed by the fast moving Rapti and Manhari rivers. The Ranas had built a fort-like structure to entertain British dignitaries from India and national figures from Kathmandu. This is where the British viceroy and commanders from Calcutta were invited to hunt tigers. They feasted on roasted wild boar and venison and enjoyed evening bonfires entertained by tribal dancers. Liquor flowed upward from India to Nepal while delicacies were supplied by the Nepalese rulers.

The old fort of the Sauraha camp still exists, although in a dilapidated condition. Some scholars and historians of Nepalese origin proposed that Nepal's sovereignty was in part protected by this type of carefully cultivated soft diplomacy. Of course, there were many other factors, including Nepal's agreement to supply

Gurkha soldiers for the British Indian Army and the fact the country was viewed as being so remote and inaccessible that it might not be worth the trouble to invade and conquer.

The midsection of Chitwan had miles and miles of grassland, which was later used for the Rapti Valley project. The two co-directors of the project, Malla and John Holiday, the project's USOM director, both had a significant impact on my life.

The western part of Chitwan is known for an abundance of rhinoceros. It was also known in the past for being rife with bandits and robbers, who entered Chitwan and forcibly collected money and food before disappearing across the border into India again. An American entrepreneur established a well-known forest resort in the area called Tiger Tops, which brought the first wave of tourists into the previously unknown area.

I worked for three years in Rapti Valley. Some memories stand out: on the first day of my work with Mr. Holiday, my boss, the tall black man bent down to make sure that I would hear him. He said, "Boy, you are so small. Will you be able to understand what I say?"

I replied with my understated humor, "Sir, I will understand. We will be a perfect example of the English phrase 'the long and the short of it.'"

He burst out laughing. This first meeting laid the foundation for our smooth working relationship.

There was another incident that is etched in my memory. One extremely hot afternoon, Mr. Holiday asked me to go with him for a cool swim in the nearby Narayani River. I picked up my towel and joined him in his Jeep. It was around noon, and sunrays were simmering all around us. After 15 minutes of driving on the forested path, we reached the riverbank.

Mr. Holiday parked his Jeep in an isolated place. I noticed a group of women washing their clothes at a distance. To my horror, I also noticed that Mr. Holiday had taken his clothes off and had proceeded to jump into the river. I shouted at him, "Don't go into the river completely naked!" He ignored my plea and began to splash in the cool water of the river. I also went for a swim but kept my shorts on.

Within half an hour, I noticed a large group of males marching toward us with wooden sticks in their hands. They looked vicious, and their faces looked grim. Instinctively, I felt great danger ahead, so I swam toward Mr. Holiday to warn him that he should not come out of the water until I shouted, "All clear."

Then I came out of the river, wrapped a towel around myself, and walked briskly towards the group of angry males. Sounding innocent, I asked them the purpose of their walking along the riverbank at this time of tropical heat.

At least half a dozen men started shouting, "Has this black man no shame?! He knew our women were washing clothes there. He ignored our culture and jumped wildly into the river. We will beat the shit out of him!"

I pleaded with them that he did not intend to violate our cultural norms. I said that they bathed naked in his country as they did in Japan. They growled at me and asked, "Did you tell him that in Nepal, you are forbidden to be naked in public, especially in the presence of women?"

After half an hour of accusations by them and pleas from me, it was agreed that it was a mistake and that I would ensure it would not happen in the future. The group dissolved slowly. I went into the river and shouted, "All clear, Mr. Holiday; you can come out now!" Thus, we avoided a major incident arising out of a cultural misunderstanding that afternoon.

CHAPTER 11

A New Beginning

A N election result thousands of miles away from Kathmandu led to another upheaval in my life. After I had worked for three years in Chitwan District, we were shocked, or happy, depending upon the political orientation, by the election of John F. Kennedy as the young president of the United States. He had defeated Richard Nixon. It created ripples of joy as well as shock among the staff of USOM at Rabi Bhawan. We also felt somewhat uneasy in Chitwan district as gradual but distinct changes took place in USAID policy to Nepal.

A few weeks after the election result was announced, Mr. Holiday, my boss, had a talk with me. He told me that his days were limited as a senior US official in Nepal. He was a Republican; the new Democratic administration would make personnel changes. He said that I was too young to understand the intricacies of, and the infighting in, the US bureaucracy. He advised me to explore the prospect of employment at the Central Secretariat, Singha

Durbar, in Kathmandu. I laughed and told him, "No one will give me a job there."

"I've spoken about you with Krishna B. Malla. You should meet him and tell him you are interested in working in Singha Durbar."

As he had anticipated, Mr. Holiday was recalled to Washington, D.C., and major staff changes occurred in the US Mission in Kathmandu. With strong letters of recommendation from Mr. Holiday and K. B. Malla, I managed to get a job in Nepal's civil service. I became a "section officer" in the Ministry of Agriculture, attached to the Department of Cooperatives, responsible for scholarships and external contacts.

Working in Kathmandu was very different from working in Chitwan. In Kathmandu, I experienced the bureaucratic tug-of-war between various ministries and came to understand the strategic need to watch one's back and, above all, to please both political figures and administrative superiors. Nepal was inundated in those days with offers of foreign scholarships and short-term training courses abroad. More than 31 countries and aid agencies offered scholarships by the donor countries working in Nepal. I was responsible for managing and coordinating these programs. The Colombo Plan scholarship offered the largest number of training courses and opportunities to study abroad. The US government offered subject-specific scholarships as well as academic ones, including the prestigious Fulbright.

The British Council also offered various training opportunities for Nepal's civil servants and students. The government of Israel ran a vigorous program of educational exchange through its embassy in Kathmandu. Also, there were sector-specific, specialized training programs offered by agencies of the United Nations, including the Food and Agriculture Organization, the World Health Organization, and UNESCO, which was dedicated to the preservation of cultural heritage. I had to liaise and coordinate with the ministries of finance, foreign affairs, and education. Consequently, I was fully engaged in the internal administration both in the secretariat and a section of foreign embassies concerned with educational programs.

My new job in Kathmandu gave me satisfaction, but it also gave rise to financial problems. I rented an apartment thanks to a friend from my Chitwan days. I then invited my sister Satyavati, with whom I had lived in Banaras, and who now was staying in our ancestral home in Govindpur, to come and settle in Kathmandu. By now she was widowed. She had four growing children, two girls and two boys in urgent need of schooling. I arranged for their admission to a local school in Kathmandu, and my household now consisted of six members.

At the time, there was a belief in Nepali society, entirely mistaken, that a person employed by the government could easily facilitate their friends' and relatives' employment. Despite my advice to the contrary, two of my eldest sister's grown sons came and lived with us. Thus, within a few months of my employment in Kathmandu, I had to support an extended family of eight people in a small apartment. Later, I learned that eight is a lucky number in China. But in my case, it became a source of misery. As a section officer, my monthly salary was less than ten rupees per day. It was not easy for me to house, clothe, educate, and feed eight people. It became obvious to me that this lifestyle was unsustainable.

But I got a lucky break again. Narayan Banskota, for whom I had handled small chores in Banaras when he was the editor of *Pragati* magazine, and who appreciated my literary bent, was now director general of the Department of Government Publications. One day, I went to see him. He offered me tea and the luxurious brand of cigarettes he used to smoke, either Rothmans or 555. As I sipped my tea, I couldn't restrain myself from saying, "No cigarettes for me, please, as even rice and lentils are difficult to procure." His face became serious and focused. When I told him about my household situation, he looked worried. He knew my late brother-in-law and my sister Satyavati.

"Well, my department has to publish some 'highbrow' political pamphlets within 15 days, at the instruction of the Royal Palace." He asked me, "Satish Babu, can you do it in 15 days?"

"Of course!" I quickly replied. "I will submit a draft manuscript within seven days, but I need a 50-percent advance now. As a man from Banaras, you know," I said, "*bhuke pet na bhajan Gopala*" (a hungry stomach is not able to sing the praises of Lord Krishna).

He guffawed and asked his secretary to call the accountant and instruct him to bring 2,000 rupees from the contingency budget. Within less than an hour of my meeting Mr. Banskota, I was richer by more than six months' salary. While we were waiting for the accountant, we struck a deal. He needed someone who could write in English about Nepal's developments. I agreed to write, but with one proviso: I didn't want my name printed in full.

"No problem. We even publish anonymous pamphlets!" he enthusiastically reassured me. Thus, my friendship and old journalistic connection with the director of the department became a lifeline for my survival.

The first pamphlet was called "From Parliament to Panchayat." Panchayat was a system of political control by Late King Mahendra to replace the democratic, election-based system of parliament. Mr. Banskota later told me that it bought me 15 minutes of fame and generated curiosity about the author, who could cite Shakespeare at one end and the German sociologist Karl Mannheim on the other, in support of the Panchayat system of governance. Though rewarding in the short run, I realized instinctively that it was neither a viable nor a desirable career in the long run.

One of the unanticipated pleasures of working for the government, I found out, was the opportunity to go abroad at the government's expense. If one was nominated to participate in meetings or take part in an international training program, the government paid for a modest daily allowance and clothing allowance for a suit and tie.

Many government bureaucrats looked forward to such opportunities to travel. I benefited twice during my four years of employment in Kathmandu: I was offered the opportunity to visit Thailand and Israel. These visits broadened my perspective on development and offered me the chance to attain my dream of learning and widening my exposure to the world.

My nomination to attend a planning workshop in Bangkok was the first occasion that I flew out of Nepali skies to the capital of Thailand. I vividly recall this journey—the orchid-wearing, ever-smiling air hostesses of Thai Airways, then upon my arrival the sultry weather and the flow of humanity in the crowded city. I was struck by how clean the city was.

The workshop was organized by the United Nations agency ECAFE (United Nations Economic Commission for Asia and the Far East) (now renamed as ESCAP).

We were housed at a hotel called Erawan at the center of the city. Next to the hotel there was a famous shrine of the Brahma, a Hindu god of creation to whom hundreds of devotees came to offer prayers and burned incense. I had never seen such a harmonious veneration by a crowd of Buddhist devotees to a Hindu god, even though I came from a Hindu kingdom where Buddha was born.

The planning workshop was chaired by a professor named Jan Tinbergen. The senior officials at ESCAP paid him special attention. During the breakfast hour, delegates from various countries would crowd around him. After a couple of mornings, I noticed that this humble-looking, aged professor loved eating slices of papaya for breakfast. I was also very fond of papaya, so one morning I got to his table before others surrounded him. After a little talk about the varieties of papaya in India, Nepal, and Thailand, in my innocent and yet brash manner, I asked him, "What are you a professor of? And at which university?"

The gentle professor smiled and told me, "The Netherlands School of Economics at Rotterdam." I bandied about the names of a few economists I knew, and he patiently listened. He asked me about my formal education.

"I have a bachelor of arts!" I told him proudly. The professor again gave me a kind smile and, noticing his good mood, I quickly asked him, "May I join you for papaya breakfast for the next few mornings?"

"Of course!" he replied.

A few days before the workshop ended, the professor asked me, "Satish, would you like to study further? And if so, in which country?"

"Professor, I have a great wish to continue my studies. Which country depends on funding and scholarship. As you know, I cannot afford to pay for it, and as the English idiom goes, beggars cannot be choosers."

He smiled and said, "Satish, if you ever decide to study in Western Europe, please drop me a line." He handed me his card with his personal telephone number scribbled on it. This card turned out to be my passport and ticket to a decade of studying in the Netherlands. Much later, I learned that Jan Tinbergen was the first economist awarded a Nobel Prize.

After returning to Nepal, I submitted my report to the government. There were three parts to the report. One was more bureaucratic: the date of departure, the date of return, the place where I stayed in Bangkok, the number of participants etc. The second part consisted of problems of human resource development as then viewed by experts from Asia; the third part was the recommendation of the conference. I was told later that it was appreciated, particularly for my emphasis on the need for human resource development in Nepal.

My second journey was a mesmerizing trip to Israel for three months' training on the role of organized labor in national development. This program was jointly sponsored by the International Labor Organization (ILO), based in Geneva, and the Israeli government.

At the time, the government of Israel had a rather weak and

isolated presence in South Asia. India was committed to the policy of nonalignment, and its leanings were toward Egypt and its charismatic president, Nasser. As a result, Israel was boycotted by India, the dominant power in South Asia. On the other hand, socialist leaders in Nepal and Burma [Myanmar] were much friendlier toward Israel's progressive government. These countries all had member parties in the Socialist International. Thus, the Israeli embassy in Rangoon and the consulate in Kathmandu were very active in promoting educational and cultural exchanges. The Israeli government offered numerous scholarships to the officials of the various ministries of the government of Nepal.

I was nominated in 1963 for an ILO–Israeli training program in Tel Aviv. A senior official, Rabindra Nath Sharma, who later became deputy prime minister of Nepal, was also nominated. Both of us traveled to Tel Aviv via Beirut because there was no direct flight to Israel from Nepal or India. The glitter and glamour of Beirut made such a deep impression on me that I vowed to visit Lebanon again—not as a transit passenger, but as a full-fledged tourist.

My three months' sojourn in Israel opened up new cultural vistas and a deeper awareness of Jewish history and culture. Before that visit, I had had little appreciation for the Jewish quest for a homeland in the ancient kingdom of Solomon. I had read the Bible but had not realized the connections between the three Abrahamic religions—Judaism, Christianity, and Islam.

The hostel in Tel Aviv where I stayed had a large library. It gave me a unique opportunity to learn the history and culture of Jewish people in Eastern Europe. It also helped me understand the unending series of persecutions, pogroms, and expulsions they had suffered. The biographies of David Ben-Gurion, Theodor Herzl, Abba Eban, and Golda Meir helped me understand the contribution of Eastern European cultural figures to the founding of Israel. The wave of European settlers coming to Palestine, followed by mass migrations of Jews from the Middle East and Africa, became evident to me in the changing demography of cities like East Jerusalem, the port city of Haifa, and the cosmopolitan Tel Aviv.

In retrospect, I think the pre-1967 era was qualitatively a more idealistic society than the Israel of today. The greed for ever more land and obsession to dominate the neighborhood was less evident then, if not nonexistent. Before the war of 1967, Egypt almost toppled the-then Israeli government. But the Israeli army was able to defeat the Arab strategy of liberation of Palestine. It let to a vast expansion of Israel controlled Arab territories and brought about a change in the Israeli government strategy of peace with the Arabs. I remember and cherish certain unforgettable experiences I had during my stay there.

I was pleasantly surprised that Saturday, the weekly holiday in Nepal, was also the Sabbath, the day of rest, in Israel. Only much later in my life did I understand the significance of Sabbath blessings among the Jewish people.

I had learned swimming in the Ganges in Banaras by holding onto the tail of a buffalo. I still remember my astonishment at swimming in the Dead Sea. I was an unsinkable float. I tried several times to swim under the water, but every time I was pushed to the surface by the salt-laden water.

My visit to Jerusalem made a lifelong impression on me, as a city unique in the world. First, massive stones of pale-white color are the foundation of Jewish architecture. Having come from the valley of Kathmandu, which abounds with stone and woodwork, I was deeply moved by the beauty of the city. The black-cap-wearing Orthodox Jews reminded me of Nepali Brahmin priests, with the black circumference formed on their shaven scalps and only tufts of black hair left on the top of their heads (called *Tuppi* in Nepali).

A visit to the Holocaust memorial and museum Yad Vashem is an experience no one can forget. I had the privilege of visiting the Anne Frank Museum in Amsterdam later in my life. During my journeys through West Germany, Czechoslovakia, and Austria, I visited places of Nazi atrocities. But invariably I was reminded of the Holocaust museum in Jerusalem.

I had requested that our program organizers arrange for me to visit and stay at a kibbutz.

When asked if I had a preference, I said, "Degania Alef." I had read that it was the first kibbutz organized by Ben-Gurion. My request was granted, and I had the pleasure and privilege of spending a week there. I picked apples from the orchard, cleaned the kitchen, looked after kids around the swimming pool, and sang "Hava Nagila" in the community dance hall. It was an unforgettable week.

In our multicultural hostel in Tel Aviv, there was an Israeli Palestinian boy named Mahmoud who was from Haifa; he worked in the kitchen. We had participants in our seminar from Brazil, Cameroon, Kenya, Iran (this was during Mohammad Reza Shah's rule), Tanzania, and Thailand. I would see Mahmoud in the corridor and sometimes in the pantry. I used to smile and greet him, and we became friendly. One day I asked him jokingly, "Mahmoud, will you invite me to your home in Haifa to meet your parents? I have never visited an Arab home."

He was startled, and after a long pause, he said, "Let me talk to my elders. And you should inform the institute authorities of your wish to visit an Arab home."

After a few days, Mahmoud asked me to go with him to Haifa. We traveled together by bus. That Friday evening, I experienced warm and profuse Arab hospitality. There were various delicacies, including pilaf and roasted lamb. There was haunting Arabic music. It was a record of Umm Kulthum's songs. Mahmoud noticed that I was enchanted by the quality of her voice and sad strands of her music though I did not know Arabic. He informed me that she was an Egyptian singer most popular all over the Arab world. That's how I was introduced to the renowned diva.

Upon my return to Tel Aviv, I came to know that many Jewish settlers from Europe and North Africa were quite fond of Maria Callas, Umm Kulthum, and Edith Piaf, who was known for her iconic signature song called *Je Ne Regrette Rien*.

Mr. Yaakov, our program coordinator, asked me smilingly, "How was the roasted lamb meat in Haifa?"

I was startled by his question and asked, "How do you know about the lamb?"

"We know; we know," he said, still smiling.

Mahmoud later told me that the Israeli government and their various institutions kept an attentive eye on foreigners who visited Arab households. It was my first exposure to Israel's monitoring of its Arab population. My time in Israel expanded my cultural horizons and my understanding of the two ancient civilizations, Jewish and Islamic, that were struggling for a home and an identity in Israel.

In the Hindu scriptures, I had read the story of the Pandavas and the Kauravas in the epic called *Mahabharata*, in which the grandchildren of a single grandfather fought a savage war. One group of grandchildren would not give up control of five villages. Therefore, the Pandavas, the grandchildren deprived of land, fought the dominant grandchildren, called the Kauravas. Consequently, millions of soldiers and untold numbers of innocent people were killed before the Pandavas finally overthrew the rule of the Kauravas. The ongoing violence between the Jews and the Palestinians reminds me of that ancient epic. Two stubborn children of Palestine appeared to me to be repeating the story of *Mahabharata*. I returned to Kathmandu wiser but melancholy in my heart.

I was full of ideas from what I learned in Israel. In my report to the government, I concluded that we could apply drip irrigation in the western, arid parts of Nepal, diversify crops, and implement better marketing techniques. The entire field of water management had great potential for cooperation with Israel.

I did not know at the time that a political colleague who had gone to Israel with me had recommended with great enthusiasm the establishment of kibbutzim in rural areas in Nepal. A few weeks after our return, I was invited to participate in a meeting organized by the Minister of Agriculture and Rural Development. In a seminar-like setting and in the presence of dozens of senior officials, the agenda for Nepal's cooperation with Israel was discussed. I noticed there was a large degree of consensus on the establishment of a couple of kibbutzim in western and central Nepal. To my bewilderment, I heard they had already selected a few districts.

The Minister of Agriculture and Rural Development asked me to give my opinion, as I had spent a week in Ben-Gurion's kibbutz. I think I spoke for less than an hour, during which I demolished the feasibility of this form of agricultural organization in Nepal. Our Hindu tradition and culture led us to seek individual initiatives for salvation (*moksha*), but the kibbutz demanded participation in pursuit of community uplift. Equally importantly, there would not be a common ideology to unite Nepali people like the ideological unity of the kibbutz did in Israel. The acute problem created by the caste system would also be a major hindrance. For instance, Nepalese citizens belonging to the Brahmin caste are prohibited to plough the land. Some people of lower castes are banished from offering drinking water to the members of the upper caste.

I was surprised that the other participants began to suggest that I was "anti-progress." As their recriminations against me increased in volume, I suggested that we should invite an Israeli expert, preferably someone who lived in a kibbutz, to give an independent assessment. The minister told me that the government had decided to request a consultant to help establish kibbutzim in Nepal. I requested, in turn, that even before a consultant was called, we ought to have asked for someone from the Israeli embassy to give us a frank opinion. The minister assured me he would personally talk with the Israeli ambassador.

The meeting ended without a firm decision and with many participants giving me accusing glares. I was not informed about future developments, and after a few months, a senior official told me that I had sabotaged the initiative. I also began to feel my colleagues and friends in the ministry starting to avoid me and, often, isolating me from meetings and seminars.

After the fiasco over kibbutzim in Nepal, I began to withdraw from my colleagues and felt quite alone. There was an increasing economic burden at home, and I felt a growing sense of repetitive, grinding work at the office. I felt I was becoming a pencil-pusher, a glorified clerk living in a bureaucratic tunnel with no light nor exit in sight. After a boring and repetitive cycle of activities in the office, I would go to the American Cultural Center on New Road. I would pick up a book or two, wander around town, and walk back to my apartment to face the worries and concerns of my family of eight members. After a quick dinner of traditional Nepali dishes, I would retire to my bedroom and get lost in the wide cosmos of the Voice of America or the BBC. I would make friends with Duke Ellington, Ella Fitzgerald, or the crooner Frank Sinatra. On the BBC, I would listen to comedians, story-reading programs, and the modular voices of news broadcasters, who would take me away to the exotic lands of Africa and Latin America. I lived in a valley in the Himalayas, but I roamed around the unseen, colorful societies of the Incas, the Aztecs, the Igbos, and the Muslim Hausa of West Africa.

There was a growing distance between my physical world and the nocturnal world of my imagination. My files ground me down during the day, but the world of books and music lifted me up at night.

I began to brood over going abroad for study as well as relocation. As I dealt with the scholarship program in the Ministry of Agriculture, I thought of sponsoring myself in a Commonwealth–British Council program. My acute yearning to get away from Nepal was constrained by two considerations:

The requirement that an applicant for a scholarship must agree to serve with the government for at least five years after his or her return. I was passionately determined not to go back to the government, so I was sure that I would not return from abroad.

My second worry was the upkeep of my family in Kathmandu. My meager salary, supplemented with occasional writing payments from the Department of Publicity, was barely sufficient for my extended family. In the event of my moving abroad, I worried about the economic consequences. These thoughts kept me in a state of animated suspense. I did, however, indicate my wish to study in the U.K. to Mr. Bright, the program officer in charge of education and training in the British Council.

Weeks passed by. The repetitive grind of dealing with paper work concerned with small matters began to sap my energy, which in turn gave rise to my despondency.

CHAPTER 12

RESTLESSNESS

A FTER four years spent working in the Central Secretariat of the government of Nepal, I felt a little worn out and disheartened by hassles in the office and the deteriorating political climate. I began to ask myself, "Is this what life has to offer?" 10:00 am to 5:00 pm in the office, always on the alert to protect myself from bureaucratic enemies. And suffering a general sense of ennui and malaise.

My intensive studies at the British Library and the American Cultural Center had given me a level of confidence to say to myself, "I am not just it. I can do something better, somewhere else."

I felt an intense urge to go on an intellectual and cultural journey to places about which I had read so much, and to imbibe the values and ethos of Western culture. Every day I felt an intense need for a pilgrimage to the lands of poets, philosophers, and painters. Indeed, I had a physical urge to have *darshan* (reverent view or experience) of the homeland of Shakespeare, the British Romantic poets, and the city of Paris in France. The concept of "the flowers of evil" fascinated me; they seemed to be the western equivalent of Lord Ganesha, who was created by the goddess Parvati out of sweat and dirt. The immortal painters of the Netherlands—Vermeer, Van Gogh, Rembrandt, and dozens of others—called out to me for a special viewing of their paintings. Stories of the Vikings' exploits reminded me of the stories of the *Mahabharata*.

Going to Europe was not simply an exercise in getting qualifications and credentials—rather, it was a sacred means of emancipation. So I began to devise ways to leave Kathmandu while keeping a measure of my dignity. The program officer at the British Council appeared to me almost as an avatar, a god-sent angel. He offered me a two-year scholarship for study in the United Kingdom. After being invigorated by these two years abroad, I was, in theory, supposed to come back and serve in the Nepalese bureaucracy. I had no intention of doing so.

The socialist emperors had no clothes. These secular gods miserably failed. At the other end of the political pendulum, I recall the intellectual arrogance of a Catholic president of the United States that led to the country's criminal involvement in Vietnam. His mistake also planted the seeds of the decline of the United States' moral authority and leadership. And across the aisle, the legacy of Lincoln has degenerated into inane tweets and narrow-minded Trumpism.

These twists and turns and a jaundiced view of morality remind me of a poetic couplet, popular in the Hindi speaking world. Kabir Das, a Sufi poet who lived Banaras, sang in frustration:

"*Chaltee ko gaddi kahe, phate doodh ko khoyaa / Rangi ko narangi kahe dekh Kabira roya.*"

"They call a moving vehicle stuck / Separated milk, for making sweets, they call lost / The most colorful orange fruit they call colorless / Look, Kabir is crying!"

CHAPTER 13

A MORTAL BLOW

IT was a winter afternoon, with the glow of sunlight gradually fading away. I was at my desk chatting with some colleagues. The clerk attached to my director's office came in and informed me that there was an urgent message from Bir Hospital—the only hospital in the valley—that I should go there soonest. Somewhat nonplussed and curious, I rushed to Bir Hospital.

It was a sunny afternoon. It was common in Kathmandu that small groups of people would sit on the green grass in the front yard of the hospital eating peanuts or slices of grapefruit. Before I reached the reception desk, I heard my name being shouted from the front yard of the hospital. I turned around and saw a family friend. Although his name was Bhim Bahadur, we affectionately called him "Kaila Dai," the fourth son in the family. He was a jovial fellow, always helpful to others. I asked him, "What are you doing here?"

Instead of replying, he asked me to go with him to a walled corner of the hospital. I was stunned to see my eldest nephew, Niranjan, only eighteen years old, laid out on a stretcher. Niranjan had joined the government service just one year ago to work as a clerk at the customs-check post at a place called Janakpur in southern Nepal. He had come to Kathmandu in connection with his departmental work, and he'd been staying with me for a week or so. We were happy to have him as a guest in our apartment.

He was lifeless, and I could see saliva at the corners of his mouth, with a few buzzing flies on his face. Numb with shock, I asked Kaila Dai for an explanation. "How could this happen?" I could barely process the sight in front of me. My whole body was trembling.

"He swallowed poison. He died because of it. Your neighbor brought him here, but it was too late."

As there was no one around to claim the body, it was laid out in the front yard. It was sheer coincidence that Kaila Dai had come to visit an acquaintance being treated in the hospital. He saw Niranjan lying on the stretcher, informed the hospital that he knew the boy, then arranged to send a message to me.

In the meantime, he completed the three legal procedures required: the identification of the body, the establishment of legal possession of the dead body, and the disposal of the body in accordance with the faith of the deceased.

I was stunned, almost paralyzed. I had never seen death at close quarters. This was my first encounter. A feeling of helplessness overwhelmed me. I asked Kaila Dai, "Why did he do it?"

Being a practical man, many years my senior, he said, "Don't worry about why he did it; let us agree on urgent tasks we need to do now. First, we must find at least four people to carry the body to Arya Ghat. Second, we need to arrange to buy enough logs to burn the body. Third, we must find and appoint a Hindu *pundit* to complete the rituals. All these steps require considerable amounts of money." He looked at me expectantly.

I told him my immediate concern was to find four able-bodied people to carry Niranjan's body to the burning ghat. After some discussion, we agreed I would somehow arrange 2,000 rupees in cash, while he would complete the other processes. My ears still ring with the hospital guard's shouts, "*Murda uthaunus! Murda uthaunus!*" "Remove the dead body! Remove the dead body!"

Kaila Dai insisted that I meet him at Arya Ghat with money for all the payments we needed to make. He would complete the other arrangements. I rushed back to my finance officer to make an urgent plea for an advance against my salary. By this time, everyone in the office had become of aware of the suicide in my family. So getting the money was not a problem, although the finance officer did caution me that it would take a couple of months for me to pay off the loan. With the money in my pocket, I went to the burning ghat, where Kaila Dai was eagerly waiting for me.

The suicide of my nephew Niranjan had a depressive, almost slow poisoning effect on me. I began to struggle with two inter-related speculations. First, why did he do it? And second, was I deficient in looking after my kith and kin? There were external unanticipated pressures. Niranjan's parents, my eldest sister and her husband, came to Kathmandu. I tried to console them to the extent I could, but I sensed an undercurrent of blame toward me. My brother-in-law kept saying that he would have kept his son in their village if he had had even an inkling of his son's frustration.

The other nephew who was staying with me, Niranjan's brother Girish, went home (I suspect at the request of his father) and pursued his legal studies in a nearby town.

The sadness and sorrow at home and the unending bureaucratic tug-of-war in the office persuaded me to exile myself from Nepal. The only impediment was the loan I had taken, which would take at least six months to repay. I decided to use this time carefully to select a British scholarship in keeping with my job in the government. I opened a channel of negotiations with Mr. Bright at the British Council. Fortunately for me, there was one scholarship in the field of agricultural economics at the University of Nottingham awarded under the Commonwealth study program. With Mr. Bright, I discussed informally the possibility of using it myself to study in the U.K. He readily agreed, subject to my nomination by the government of Nepal. As there was almost half a year before my possible departure for the U.K., I assured him that I would resolve other administrative hurdles such as the duration of my leave from the government.

Each government and its bureaucracies devise specific sets of limits and boundaries. In my case, they appeared to be major hurdles. The first was, as I mentioned, that I was required to commit that after my return from the U.K., I would serve for five years with the government. It was a general rule for all scholarship-holders.

The process of getting government approval to study abroad, especially for a master's degree, turned out to be equally complicated. K. B. Malla, whom I knew in Chitwan, as he had been promoted as the Chief Secretary of His Majesty's Government of Nepal. I had worked under him, and his appreciation of my past work turned out to be an obstacle. He tried to persuade me to stay and work in Nepal by offering the prospect of a promotion to a more senior role. After a few weeks of my lobbying and advocacy, he agreed to send my file with his recommendation to the Minister of Development, one Mr. Bishwa Bandhu Thapa. He was a rising politician much trusted by the king. As my luck would have it, I knew him well from the days of my work in Rapti Dun. In those days, he used to appear suddenly in the evenings at my wooden cottage for dinner and political talk. I distinctly remember the cotton carry-bag that he used to hang around his shoulder. It included toiletries and a small towel, called a *gamchha* in Nepali.

He liked me as a person and appreciated my work. I found out, after my return from Israel, that he was instrumental in sending me there and wanted me to head up the first kibbutz in Nepal. However, his goodwill toward me became a major hurdle to my obtaining the British scholarship. Four weeks after K. B. Malla sent my file to Thapa's office, I sought an appointment with my friendly minister. In keeping with tradition in those days, he offered me tea and biscuits; he asked about my health and the wellbeing of my widowed sister; and then he asked me, with a smile on his face, the purpose of my meeting with him. "To accelerate your decision regarding my file," I replied.

He responded with a smile that he would not approve it. Taken aback and suddenly short-tempered, I asked him the reason for it. I still remember the Nepali idiom he recited: "Satish, 'one cannot sail two boats simultaneously.' You cannot be a rising civil servant with a great future ahead of you and also aspire to be an academic. Why do you want to go for further study?"

I was so angry it took me a few minutes to restrain myself. Then I replied, with a great deal of formality, "Honorable minister, thank you for reminding me of the Nepali idiom. May I also recite another that is more relevant in my case? 'It is said that a thick mustache cannot prevent a hungry mouth from eating.'"

The minister laughed out loud and said, "Don't be angry."

I got up and left his chamber. A week or two later, the Office of the Chief Secretary called to give me the good news that the minister had approved my file. I silently thought to myself, "And my destiny."

I arranged with the Ministry of Agriculture to give my half-salary (which was paid to all civil servants going abroad) to my sister Satyavati.

The next day, I called the British Council and told Mr. Bright that I wanted to finalize my itinerary, with three weeks in transit spread over five days in Beirut, five days in Athens, five days in Rome, and four days in London before reaching the University of Nottingham. He was taken aback at my request and asked me who would pay my expenses for this period. I replied that I would do so with my own funds. His typical British response was to ask me to send him a note with the details of my sojourn in these places. I readily agreed.

I had carefully chosen the three cities to visit on my way to

London. I wanted to see the great urban centers of Mediterranean civilization: the splendor of Beirut and the nearby ruins of Baalbek; Athens, the fountainhead of Western philosophy and the first place to have democratic governance in history; and Rome, the metropolis of the first global empire. I was keen to visit these cities before reaching London, lest I need to return to Nepal after the completion of my studies.

There were two excellent guidebooks for student tourists. One was Arthur Frommer's *Europe on $5 a Day*. I understood that as a G.I. in Germany, Frommer had also written an even cheaper guidebook for a budget of $1.00 a day. How I wished I had a copy of that book! The second book was called *Let's Go to Europe*, published by a group of students in Boston. With the lifeline thrown me by these two books, I had decided to spend three weeks before reaching the U.K.

Before I left Kathmandu, I bought some miniature statues of the Buddha. One was for myself. The others were to be gifts for people I had not met yet, but whom I knew would impact my life journey.

PART 2

CHAPTER 14

BAALBEK AND BEYOND

AFTER reaching Beirut, my immediate problem was to find cheap lodgings where I could spend my days. I was lucky to find a Persian Shia taxi driver. While riding with him, I told him that almost 25 percent of the words in the Nepali language came from Farsi. My driver was astonished when I brought up the names of two Iranian poets, Omar Khayyam and Hafiz. He was delighted to find a Hindu traveler with such an appreciation of his culture. He asked me, "Why are you paying so much money for such a dilapidated lodge? If you don't mind, I have an extra room and you could stay there for a few days while you are here. It is not a fancy room, but it will be comfortable." Luck had again blessed me with the help of an angel.

My taxi driver friend was curious as to why I wished to spend five days in Beirut. I promptly replied that two days preciated by British authors such as the Romantic poet Lord Byron, and the author of the travelogue called *The Road to Oxiana*.

He was surprised again and blurted out, "How do you know about Baalbek?" I told him of my love of reading, especially travelogues. My first stop was Baalbek on account of my fascination with gods and their temples.

"Coming from Kathmandu with Hindu Buddhist and Tibetan temples, I want to see first-hand the place where Baal, the god of the sky and lord of heaven and earth, was worshipped."

"How will you travel there?"

"I've noted down the bus number from my guide book—Dr. Frommer's. Do you know it? I'm thinking of two day-trips by bus so I can see as much as possible."

British writers had compared Baalbek to the famous canyon-city of Petra in Jordan. There was an intermingling between Iranian, Arabian, and Greco-Roman styles in the architecture of the ruins. Unfortunately, Petra has been demolished beyond recognition these days, due to the internecine fight between the rulers of Syria and ISIS, and Baalbek has become a hiding place among the caves for Hezbollah fighters.

After Alexander the Great conquered the Beqaa valley, Baalbek became Heliopolis ("City of the Sun"), and after the Roman conquest of the region, several temples were dedicated to Jupiter, Bacchus, and Venus. Over time the Roman Empire declined, and now only the ruins remain. I was thrilled to see at least 24 huge blocks of limestone and three colossal megaliths. I had read that these huge stones were transported here from Aswan in Egypt. How this rose-pink granite in the temple of Jupiter was transported such a distance remains a fascinating story.

I found my decision to spend two days in Baalbek was wise because one could not view and admire all the temples and their ruins in one day. On my second day, I was lucky to find a tourist group of Scandinavians, mostly Swedes, with a competent guide explaining the intricacies of the ruins. I quietly joined the group and learned much about the historical sites.

My stay in Beirut gave me an opportunity to taste Mediterranean food again with its delightful new flavors. I remember my first bite of hummus and warm bread as I explored the street food of the city. At the end of my stay, my Lebanese host dropped me at the departure gate of Beirut International Airport. Overwhelmed by his generosity, I thanked him profusely and gave him a miniature statue of the Buddha.

After a short flight over the Mediterranean Sea, I landed in Athens. My first impression of the airport, and later of the city, was disappointing. Compared with the opulence of Beirut, Athens appeared a run-down city in decline. As I exited the airport, there was chaos. At the baggage-claim area, half a dozen or more loaders tried to grab each passenger's luggage. There were people begging or waiting for "tips." Taxi drivers shouted for fares. It all reminded me of Palam Airport in Delhi, India, from which I had recently departed. I took a cab to the Monastiraki neighborhood, where accommodations were cheap.

Once I left the airport, I was taken by Athens—its bright colors, brilliant sunshine, and the orange trees and benches shaded with vines. I was impressed by the extensive flea market at Monastiraki and found that it was a strategic starting point for undertaking a walking tour of the city. I was interested in visiting the Acropolis and its temple of Athena. I walked there through café-lined streets. The Old Acropolis Museum was an added attraction. It had three levels of exhibitions and glass floors to allow visitors to view the statues, including those recovered from the area surrounding the Parthenon, from all angles.

To me, Athens looked like a vast open-air theater. I could have spent four weeks visiting temples and archeological sites. However, in view of my limited time there and my dwindling funds, I decided to walk around the city to a few targeted loca-tions, like the Ancient Agora and the National Archaeological Museum. At the museum, I met a Greek graduate student, to whom I mentioned I was on my way to the U.K. for further study. He told me, with considerable passion, that the Anglo-Saxons had destroyed Greece. My talk with him inspired me to read more about modern Greece, not only its ancient history.

After five extremely frugal days in Greece, I left wishing I could stay longer, and vowed to return for a longer stay, which regretfully I have not been able to do. I flew out on the Italian national airline called Alitalia to the majestic city of Rome.

Rome had fascinated me since my student days in Banaras and Kathmandu. My reading about the Renaissance had given me a mental picture of Rome as a center of pilgrimage as well as of higher learning. This was also true of Banaras. Rome encompassed the capitals of two countries, Italy and the Vatican, and like Banaras, it was an ancient city with thousands of years of history. Due to its historical and cultural significance, Rome is often called *Caput Mundi*: "Capital of the World."

I had read the travelogues and diaries of European authors like Byron, Shelley, and Goethe, and they had given me some idea of Rome. Moreover, at the American Library in Kathmandu, I had watched the enormously popular film *Roman Holiday*, starring Gregory Peck and Audrey Hepburn. I was also a devoted fan of the Italian novelist Alberto Moravia, who wrote *La Romana,* a romantic novel with two beautiful women, mother and daughter, striving to make a decent life in post-Second World War Rome.

When I landed at Leonardo da Vinci Airport, I immediately felt surprisingly at home in Rome. I took a room in a hotel near Piazza Navona. After getting refreshed, I started out on foot to visit the Fontana di Trevi. There were hundreds of tourists milling around the fountain, many of them dropping coins in the water in the hopes that it would bring them to Rome again. I dropped a few coins in the fountain myself. Perhaps that's what helped me return with my wife, Sheila, a return for which I am eternally grateful.

After an hour or so, I began to explore the neighborhood for a pizzeria. Soon I found a distinct place with a long oven in which dozens of pizzas were being baked. I had a lovely feast of pizza and my first taste of Chianti, a wine that I had so far only read about in books.

The next morning, I started out to visit the Colosseum. It is said to have been able to seat 90,000 spectators. It is, indeed, a great wonder of the world. In the afternoon, I headed out to the Vatican, where I felt very fortunate to walk around Saint Peter's Square and view the Sistine Chapel. That night, I had a delicious dinner of Spaghetti alla Carbonara, a first again. I spent the next few days visiting the Catacombs, the Villa Borghese, and the National Museum. After being sated by Italian cuisine, bright green parks, and historical sites, I was airborne to London.

I was starting to get weary traveling on one pair of shoes, the soles of which were getting thinner by the day. In retrospect, I can hardly believe my foolhardy decision to spend three weeks on a total of $175.00 and without any friends or family members in the cities I visited.

When I arrived at Heathrow Airport, I was a bit worried about bureaucracy and the questions I would be asked going through customs. To my surprise, everything turned out smoothly because I had had my student visa issued in Kathmandu and my travel agent, Thomas Cook, had made room reservations from Rome.

Being a Nepali passport holder also helped me because I was not considered a "Paki." I mention this because within a month of my arrival, I realized there was an increasing level of resentment among white citizens in England at the sudden and increasing appearance of migrants from South Asia, Africa, and the Caribbean.

After checking into my hotel, I ventured out to explore my surroundings. I still have a vivid memory of that evening: the palpable, yellowish fog that blanketed the streets and squares. The flow of humanity moving silently toward the nearest Tube station. Large crowds of people walking with hats on their heads and umbrellas in their hands. This exploration led me to a small British pub where I had, for the first time, a taste of fish and chips and a glass of bitter.

I found so many things confusing. Penny, farthing, shilling—as familiar as I was with British literature, the books had not adequately prepared me to deal confidently with small coins. This led to an ever-increasing weight in my pocket.

I was familiar with British and American accents, but I had not realized that everyone in England would not sound like the BBC radio announcers, with their rounded, polished accents. The enormous range of variation in the language spoken on the street was baffling to a newcomer like me.

I have an embarrassing memory of British lingo: after paying a visit to the Nepalese Embassy on a sunny afternoon, I was walking back happily toward the Tube station. An elderly gentleman stopped me on the pavement and quietly said, "Sir, your fly is open." I was puzzled and began to look around me. I did not see any flies. As the gentleman pointed his finger towards my trousers, an instinctive understanding flashed in my mind. I thanked him and ran ahead in my embarrassment.

During my brief stay in London, I visited some tourist spots like Hyde Park; Speakers' Corner; the famous River Thames; the Serpentine River; the British Library; and Buckingham Palace for the changing of the guard, where I was happy to see many Gurkha soldiers marching smartly.

The visit to the Charles Dickens Museum moved me. I knew that he had written vividly about social inequality four years earlier than Karl Marx wrote his seminal *Communist Manifesto*.

CHAPTER 15

NOTTINGHAM

AFTER three days of sightseeing and visits, I went by train to Nottingham. Being in the Midlands, the city looked a little drab, but the university's surroundings were quite pleasant. I was happy to find many overseas students. My roommate was a Jamaican by the name of Jimmy Braidweth; we became fast friends.

I became friends with another student too. He was from Fiji. His full name was Naand Bahadur, but he insisted that everyone should call him "Naand." After a few weeks he mentioned to me that his mother was Nepali. He had brought a brooch shaped like the small curved Nepalese knife called *khukuri*. Occasionally he would wear it on the lapel of his jacket.

These two friends educated me about the colonial histories of their countries. It was interesting to hear from Jimmy and Naand that many Indian laborers were imported to their home countries to cultivate sugarcane. Naand mentioned that Fiji had developed over time the largest ethnically Indian minority, but the local government controlled by the military and the tribal chiefs did not allow Indians to participate in the political process. Consequently, the Indo-Fijian minority developed the tourism sector. Many Australians, New Zealanders, and overseas Chinese visited Fiji as tourists. In fact, tourism had become the pillar of the economy.

I learned from Jimmy that an increasing level of resentment was taking hold in the U.K. against black and brown people. A group of young whites called "skinheads" banded together to attack "people of color."

Jimmy introduced me to the novels of V. S. Naipaul, notably *A House for Mr. Biswas*. I was so taken in by his writing that I bought and read almost all the books written by him. I will be grateful forever to Jimmy for taking me to London's largest street festival, The Notting Hill Carnival. Every summer Notting Hill celebrates Afro-Caribbean culture. There are grand parades with colorful floats. Different troupes of dancers follow them with steel bands. Once the floats and the dancers have moved on, residents and viewers are encouraged to join in the dancing. To me, a newcomer to the Carnival, the sights and sounds were stunning and unforgettable. I regret that I could not afford to buy a camera in those days. Thus, I missed the chances to capture so much beauty and vitality.

I was fascinated by the city of Nottingham for a number of reasons, including its proximity to Sherwood Forest and its importance to my reading mind as the birthplace of D.H. Lawrence, the author best known for writing *Lady Chatterley's Lover*. It was censored in the U.K. and banned in the United States for many decades. D.H. Lawrence also introduced me to the vivid and colorful history of Mexico depicted in his novel *The Plumed Serpent*.

I was enrolled in the University of Nottingham's Department of Economics, with specialization in agricultural economics. The coursework at the university emphasized economic theory as well as concrete policies. We read the works of Adam Smith, David Ricardo, Thomas Malthus, and John Maynard Keynes. In addition, we studied the reasons for the fragmentation of agricultural land in Asian societies as contrasted with the consolidation of land in European and Australian farming families. The lectures of Colin Clark, the famous agricultural economist, and guest lectures by Swedish economist Eric Jacobi added spice to my curriculum. Professor Clark had done considerable research into the problems of small farmers and fragmented land holdings in South and Southeast Asia, especially Java and Bali in Indonesia. In contrast to Western farms and the European farming system, smallholders in rural Asia divided their land into small pieces. The Asian legal system was to award land and land-based properties equally to all male children in a household. Consequently, landholdings became small and economically unviable, and led to increasing poverty in rural areas.

There were three major passions and hobbies among British university students in the early 1960s: sports, especially soccer, cricket, and American heavyweight boxing; music, especially the Beatles and political songs; and, of course, political activism.

I am not a sports person, so I did not care much about weekly soccer games boosted by bets and lottery tickets. There was a huge football stadium in Nottingham. The students were most loyal supporters of the Sherwood football team. I can be quite introverted, so I did not participate with the passion and frenzy of my British colleagues. But on my walks, I explored Sherwood Forest, renowned the world over for the exploits of my hero Robin Hood.

I do remember, though, the historic boxing match between Cassius Clay, later known as Muhammad Ali, and Sonny Liston. My friends Jimmy and Naand took me along to the TV room in the hostel. I am a rather short guy, so they maneuvered to place me on a chair nearer to the TV. The television age had not yet reached India and Nepal, so I was curious about the black-and-white magic box, the television set, as much as about the impending match.

There was a deep silence in the room full of students. The promoters were encouraging and boosting their champions in the opposite corners of the ring. The match began. In what felt like only a minute, the big and bulky Sonny Liston was flat on the floor and, as the saying goes, biting the dust. I did not know what had happened. The room exploded with cheers. A bit puzzled, I asked Jimmy, "What is going on?"

He replied, "It was the fastest knockout, man—unbelievable!"

I did not know a thing about boxing. Gradually, over a period of time, I began to love the game of boxing and watched all the matches of Muhammad Ali.

The 1960s were a period of musical renaissance. Stage-based music bands began to sprout up all over Britain. Chief among them were the Beatles, popularly known as the "Liverpool Lads." There was loud music of Caribbean singers, especially from Jamaica. I was fortunate to have Jimmy as a friend. He took me along one weekend to Liverpool to listen to the Beatles. I told him I had no money to buy tickets since I was saving for my uncertain future in Europe. I still recall his youthful response: "There is no problem, man. I already bought two tickets as I knew you would find some excuse for not going with me!"

He informed me further that one of his aunts had an apartment there. "We will spend one night at her place, that will save money for both of us." I was touched by his gesture and thanked him profusely. Thanks to Jimmy, I was able to attend the only live Beatles show of my life and taste his aunt's delicious Jamaican cuisine, highlighted by goat curry and plantains.

It was also a period of political turmoil in the U.K. and other Western democracies. The prime minister, Harold Macmillan, had announced "winds of change" blowing across Africa. France had been caught in a quagmire in Algeria until 1962. There were increasingly vocal protests and rallies to end apartheid in South Africa. American intervention in Vietnam was beginning to cloud the hopes of Lyndon Johnson's ambitious domestic agenda. Above all, the Cold War between Russia and the United States had reached a boiling point, giving rise to the possibility of the nuclear annihilation of mankind.

Against this terrible scenario of mutual destruction, some prominent British scientists led by the philosopher Bertrand Russell started a movement against nuclear proliferation. Thus, the Committee for Nuclear Disarmament, CND, came into being. It was my good luck that I was able to participate in some of the organization's political activities and rallies in London.

My attendance at political meetings and weekend marches in London and nearby cities was noted by the university's authorities. One day, as I was coming out of class, the registrar of the university caught up with me. He gave me some friendly advice. As I was on a British government scholarship, I was expected not to participate in political activism. I thanked him and took his cautionary advice. Instead of extracurricular activities, I began to read books by such authors as Frantz Fanon, Régis Debray, Albert Camus, and Jean-Paul Sartre. These authors expanded my mental horizon and gave an analytical experience of the ground level realities in many Third World countries.

While still at the university, I began to be worried about my future. I had brought Jan Tinbergen's card with me to Nottingham, and I wrote to him in the second year of my studies to remind him of our meeting in Bangkok and his kind assurance to help facilitate my studies in the Netherlands.

I had written him in early February 1965, hoping that I might hear some news before the summer holidays. Months passed by; I had no news. I was increasingly worried, so I contacted my friend Hans Ollman, the editor of the monthly magazine published by the International Co-operative Alliance. I had met him in Delhi during his participation in one of the workshops held there. I visited him a couple of times in London on weekends and academic holidays. Hans and his second wife, Catherine, had become good friends of mine.

I visited Hans one weekend in the month of April 1965 and unburdened my worries. I told him that I did not want to return to Nepal. I mentioned my letter to Jan Tinbergen and said, rather confidently, that I expected a positive reply by the end of August, as the courses in the Netherlands began in early September. It was a gamble on my part.

In early June, I received a rather bulky envelope from The Hague. The letter in the envelope gave me the happy news that I was admitted to a postgraduate course called "National Development" at the International Institute of Social Studies. It also informed me that I had been awarded a Dutch government scholarship and that I should contact Miss Coopman in the office of Dutch Technical Assistance, a department in the Ministry of Foreign Affairs. I was thrilled; my joy knew no bounds for the next week or so. I shared the news with my two university friends and with my dear friends Hans Ollman.

My exhilaration at the prospect of studying in the Netherlands was tinged with an unspoken fear. What if the British government should decide to deport me to Nepal after the completion of my studies? I had heard that a few students who had come to England on similar scholarships had been coerced to return to their home countries.

I developed a devious way to forestall such an eventuality. I informed the Registrar's Office that I was going to London to say goodbye to Nepal's Ambassador and other friendly colleagues in the embassy. I did go to London and stayed for a few days with Hans Ollman. During this period, I visited the embassy, and from there, I called the secretary to the registrar of the university in Nottingham. This convinced the university authorities of my ties to the Nepalese embassy and gave them no reason to think that I might not return to Nepal.

In the meantime, Hans had arranged for my apprenticeship for three months at the German Bank in Koblenz, Germany. It was a cooperative bank with a strong training division. Hans knew the chief of the training division rather well, so thanks to Hans, I was accepted there and was paid 1,500 deutsche marks per month. This took care of my expenses, food, and accommodation effectively. These three months gave me the experience of working in Germany. I used my spare time to read the English translations of Karl Marx's writings published in the Rheinische Zeitung.

It was a pleasant coincidence that Hans Ollman had arranged for me to work in a city that I wanted to visit. My stay in Koblenz made me appreciate the taste of the Moselle wine for which the Rhineland is famous.

After my hectic but colorful stay in Nottingham and London, I found Koblenz to be a charming and placid place. Rhineland in the summer brought back memories of the Mediterranean weather of Beirut and Athens. Koblenz was sunny and lush-green, with picturesque vineyards on both banks of the mighty Rhine. There were barges carrying a variety of commodities and finished products to different destinations across Europe. Tourist boats traveled between the cities through which the Rhine flows. One weekend I took a river tour from Koblenz to Köln. I was delighted to visit the famous cathedral in Köln and happy to see the city from which cologne and other perfumes originated.

The Commerzbank had arranged a weeklong program for me to visit Bonn, the capital of West Germany. I went there and also to the Nepal Embassy, then located at Adenauer Strasse in Bonn. It was a courtesy call on my part. Our ambassador to Germany also served as ambassador to the Netherlands. My early contact with the embassy turned out to be quite helpful to me during my longer stay in Holland. I also wrote a letter of thanks and gratitude to Professor Tinbergen, and told him that I would be able to see him in Rotterdam.

CHAPTER 16

MOLENSTRAAT, THE HAGUE

I BOUGHT a railway ticket for Amsterdam after spending twelve weeks in Koblenz. On September 5, 1965, I reached The Hague, via Amsterdam. I recall that it was a cloudy afternoon with the occasional drizzle. From the central railway station, I took a cab to Molenstraat, where the Institute of Social Studies was located.

The palace at Molenstraat was architecturally beautiful. It had a large garden with centuries-old oak trees, willow trees, and what the Dutch called *goudenregen*, "golden rain," trees with bright-yellow flowers hanging to the ground. In the northeastern corner of the palace, there was a small, beautiful lake in which swans swam together, giving delightful pleasure to the onlookers and walkers-by. This secluded garden was my favorite place for summer strolls, where I could find a nook and settle down with a book.

The ensuing decade, from the fall of 1965 to August 1975, was the most fulfilling time of my life. From the autumn of 1965 to the end of 1966, I completed my academic studies, earning my Master of Social Sciences degree. This was also a period of intense student activism.

There were some unusual features of the Institute of Social Studies. In the mid-1950s, it had become fashionable among academics to advocate the need for interdisciplinary analysis of the development process, especially in the Third World. Consequently, Western democratic governments and universities began establishing institutes for the study of development as a distinct field of inquiry. The prime example of this trend was the Institute of Development Studies at Sussex in the U.K., under the leadership of Professor Dudley Sears.

The Dutch government, being practical and realistic, decided to avoid establishing multiple centers. Instead, they persuaded eleven universities in the Netherlands to establish a single institution, which would receive input from the Dutch universities and financial support from the Ministry of Education and the Ministry of Foreign Affairs. They also decided the institution would use English as the language of instruction because the Dutch language was neither global in its reach nor easy to learn in a brief period.

Furthermore, it was decided that mid-level civil servants and decision makers would be selected for admission to the proposed institute with financial support and funding from the Dutch government and multilateral agencies, such as the U.N. Professor Egbert de Vries, a distinguished administrator and academic, was invited to take the lead, and appointed as the founding rector of the Institute of Social Studies. Queen Juliana generously donated Noordeinde Palace to house the institute and provide rooms for its participants.

My first week at the institute was exhilarating. In addition to getting familiar with the course content and the morning classes, there was the joy of getting to know people from diverse backgrounds. The common room for students had a large Philips television in one corner and two billiards tables at the other end of the room. It became the hub of activity in the afternoons and early evenings, when we met, talked, and shared personal experiences.

The television was a focal point. After listening to the news, we would discuss, and sometimes argue vehemently about, atrocities around the world. Students and teachers alike were increasingly outraged about the Vietnam War. We talked about how much we admired and appreciated the young heroes of the University of California at Berkeley, the youth movement, and the flower children of the United States. The atrocities committed by the military junta in Indonesia and the never-ending conflict between India and Pakistan were also regular topics of discussion.

The political quagmire in Algeria was caused by the reluctance of France to grant full independence to Algerian citizens. The ever-increasing clamor for the independence by the Igbo people in Nigeria and pan-European support for the creation of Biafra caused rifts and factionalism between African participants and became a hot-button issue. I was interested in Algerian developments because of my appreciation of the writings of Albert Camus, who was a French Algerian by birth. I was also equally influenced by the Nigerian novelist Chinua Achebe, whose book *Things Fall Apart* is still one of my favorite novels. He was a great supporter of Biafra as a new nation, and he also wrote a book of advocacy called *There Was a Country: A Personal History of Biafra*. I, too, became a supporter of the Biafran cause.

Global issues and student movements across Western Europe created a network of friends among the students of the ISS. I was fortunate to have a core group of friends who sustained both my academic pursuits and my political activism. Dr. Jan van Lochem was a sociologist and a senior faculty member. Born in Batavia (now Jakarta), he had been arrested by the Japanese and become a prisoner of war during the Second World War. The continuing torture inflicted by the Japanese almost unhinged him except for the blessings he received in the person of Mies, a female prisoner. They fell in love and got married. She healed him from the memories of torture and his nightmares and made him almost whole again. Jan and Mies were philosopher friends and guides to me in the Netherlands. Jan had done research on the tribes and customs of Papua New Guinea. Hearing the story of his life and reading his Ph.D. thesis, which he was kind enough to share, brought us closer together.

I was among 20 participants in the national development course; it was a remarkable group of people with diverse backgrounds and differing beliefs. There was one man, Nailton Santos, who was most argumentative and voluble. He was a brilliant student. We became close friends at the ISS due to his outgoing personality, his love for Latin American music, and his skill playing the drums. He taught me how to play the bongo drum.

He had some difficulty speaking English; his accent and pronunciation were difficult to understand. For some reason, I was the only person who could understand him well. Consequently, whenever he spoke in the class, everyone would look at me and wait for me to explain the gist of what Nailton had just said. He was a big, burly black man from Bahia, in northeastern Brazil. Extroverted by nature, with a mordant and ironic sense of humor, he easily attracted attention and drew people to him.

I came to know more of his family background and troublesome past. He was a radical devoted to Marx and Mao. As a member of a Brazilian student delegation, he had visited China and met Mao, and he carried a photograph of this meeting as one of his most prized possessions. There were three heroes in his life: Pelé, Marx, and Mao. He was wildly popular with one group of students from Latin America and Africa, while being bitterly resented by others for various reasons.

My friendship with Nailton started in our early days at the ISS and spanned over two decades. He and his elder brother Milton Santos, a professor of geography at the Sorbonne, were actively associated with the Brazilian leader, Furtado. When the military junta overthrew the progressive government in Brazil, the two brothers were helped by leftist friends in France to migrate hastily to Paris. Milton was able to secure a two-year assignment at the Sorbonne, and Nailton obtained a nine-month fellowship at the Organization for Economic Co-operation and Development

(OECD). Nailton applied to study at the ISS. Although he was based in Europe, his heart was in Brazil, and he wanted to return as soon as he could without being arrested.

I often wondered about this strange friendship between us. I did not want to go back to Nepal, while Nailton wanted to return to Brazil by hook or by crook. I have so many memories of Nailton. Our favorite bar in those days was called the Crazy Horse, in Scheveningen, the entertainment district along the beach with bars, nightclubs, and dance halls. On one occasion, Nailton and I stayed until we spent our last guilder, and we suddenly realized we did not have money to pay for a taxi back to our hostel. Public transportation stopped at midnight in the Hague, and the last tram had long since departed. The prospect of spending the night on the beach, cold and shivering, sobered us up.

After some time, we saw a police car slowly doing a round. Perhaps recklessly, I raised my right arm and waved at the police car. It stopped. With affected humility and deference, I said to the policemen, "Officers, we study at the ISS. My friend and I came here to visit the beach and spend some good times here. We forgot the time of the last tram back. We do not have money to pay for a taxi. Will you please do us a favor and drop us back to our student accommodation at Molenstraat?"

They looked at us, amused.

"Okay, hop in. But next time, you must remember the last tram leaves at midnight."

Thus, Nailton and I got a free ride home thanks to the kindness of the Dutch police.

Nailton had fallen in love with a Dutch girl, Annette, who was a daughter of a rich Amsterdam family. Her father had an import-export business mainly with South Africa. Annette, being a girl of independent nature, found a job in The Hague and moved away from her parents. Nailton met her in a bar called Het Moulen, which was next to the ISS. Many participants from the Institute, including me, went there in the evenings for what I called "the evening seminar."

Annette and Nailton's friendship developed into a deep commitment, and they wanted to get married and raise a family. Annette's father, though, was vehemently opposed to his only child's getting married to someone from a different continent whose roots and family background were unknown. To a solid burgher with racist inclinations, Nailton was from an alien planet. A priest belonging to the Dutch Reformed Church tried for a few months to persuade Annette's father, but he was not successful.

Annette and Nailton decided to get married without her family's blessing. They would have a court marriage followed by a church ceremony. They had both agreed that they would like me to be Nailton's best man. I was delighted to perform the role, and immediately I started looking for a tuxedo, as was customary for the best man to wear in those functions. Much to my disappointment, I was unable to find a tuxedo in my Napoleonic size. So Nailton suggested that I wear my Nepali national dress, called *labeda surwal*, which consisted of a jacket over a long shirt with tight cotton pants and a Nepalese cap (*topi*) to top it all off.

On the wedding day, rice and confetti galore were thrown on the streets by the participants in the procession. In my national outfit, I attracted attention, curiosity, and much amusement. I was repeatedly asked, "Why are you wearing pajamas as the best man?"

CHAPTER 17

A ROYAL AUDIENCE

M Y irst two years at the ISS were eventful. Although I was a
participant there, I was also trying to watch my back and
make sure that I would not be sent back to Kathmandu. In this
context, the second secretary at the Nepalese Embassy in Bonn,
Germany, was helpful and supportive.

In early 1967, I began to get official letters from the Central
Secretariat, Singha Durbar, inquiring about the date of my return.
I replied that I did not have enough money to return and, therefore, would need more time. After receiving three such letters, I
telephoned the second secretary at the embassy in Bonn to ask
for his advice.

"I don't want to return to Kathmandu—maybe never. Yet I
keep receiving these letters. What should I do?"

"Come visit me at the Embassy. We might figure a way out."

During the first weekend of March, I took the train to Bonn
to meet with him at the embassy. I remember being somewhat

depressed as I traveled. The rose garden around the embassy building was in full bloom. It was a sunny day. Yet I had a nagging worry that the embassy would coerce me into returning to Kathmandu. When he saw me, the First Secretary of the Embassy invited me out to a German brunch at a delicatessen nearby. The German sausage and cold cuts were delicious, but I couldn't enjoy them fully as I was preoccupied with what might be the conclusion of this visit. After we ate, the First Secretary smiled broadly.

"Satish-ji, if I were you, I would send them a letter with a copy to us at the Embassy, that you do not have enough money to return, so would the government kindly send sufficient funds for your return to the embassy. Say that you will happily come back if you could receive adequate funds."

He told me that if I copied the letter to him, he would monitor my case. He informed me there was no budget for these types of funds, so he was pretty sure that the government would not send anything soon. I would then be free to continue my studies and stay in the Netherlands. I was so relieved and delighted at his idea that I invited him for a glass of wine to celebrate.

I sent the letter immediately upon my return to the Netherlands. I did not receive any more letters from the Nepalese government—a very happy outcome, in my opinion.

In late April, two more happy events affected me positively. The first was the birth of a male child in the Orange Dynasty of Queen Juliana. It was the first time that the Dutch royal family had had a male heir in a hundred years. The whole country went wild. All the major cities such as Amsterdam, Rotterdam, and The Hague were lit up, and musical programs continued for three days. There were fireworks, spontaneous musical performances on the streets and plazas, and the ISS was encouraged to close. We were all, of course, delighted at the birth of the prince and the three-day holiday.

One afternoon a few days after this historic event, I received a call from the Dutch Ministry of Foreign Affairs. A senior official asked if he could come and see me soon, preferably the next day. I agreed immediately. After the preliminaries were over, he came to the main reason for his visit.

"I am so happy to inform you, Mr. Prabasi, that your king, His Majesty King Mahendra, is going to pay an official visit at the invitation of our Queen Juliana. We have received a communication from the palace in Nepal that His Majesty would like to meet with Nepalese citizens, including students, during his visit. Her Majesty Queen Juliana will be hosting him and the Nepalese royal party at the palace in Amsterdam."

Surprised, I responded, "I would like to join the delegation of Nepali citizens who are granted an audience with our king. When is this planned? I will need to take leave from my university."

With a diplomatic smile, he replied, "It will be a one-man delegation making this courtesy call. You are the only Nepalese citizen residing in the Netherlands at this moment. I have confirmed this with our Ministry of Education and Ministry of Home Affairs."

I was stunned. And, for once, at a loss for words.

I wondered how I could get out of this situation, which, upon further reflection, was fraught with danger. A group delegation would have provided me some cover, but an individual audience with our king was another matter altogether. Whatever he asked, I would have to answer, and I knew he might be displeased with my answers. I was in a real dilemma.

I explained to my Dutch visitor that there is a popular idiom in Nepal that goes more or less like this: "A wise man does not stand in front of the king, nor behind a horse." I pretended that I did not have the appropriate national attire for such an occasion.

"It is a custom in Nepal to dress in the national *labeda surwal*, with the distinctive Nepali cap on one's head, when going to visit royalty. I'm afraid I will not be able to go, since I do not have the proper attire."

His eyes were suddenly less friendly. "We inquired at the institute about you, and the administration here informed us that you

were a great source of amusement dressed in your national clothing when you took part in one of your friends' recent wedding."

"I didn't have the cap on my head."

"Mr. Prabasi, we have already informed the palace in Nepal
that we will bring a Nepali citizen to meet the king. I have come
prepared with a small package of gifts that you should present to
the king."

He showed me the contents, which he said would be wrapped
later. There was one of my books, *The Nepalese Cooperative
Movement*, and two articles on the Vietnam War, published in
the Dutch daily, *Rotterdamsche Courant*. There was also the gold
insignia of the Institute of Social Studies. He then told me the
detailed arrangements of how I was to travel to the palace with
an escort.

My anxiety and trepidation grew by the hour, as I was an
absconder from the civil service, overdue to return to my kingdom
and start my official duties. I was also aware that our king had an
unpredictable temperament. He had been known to summarily
imprison those who offended him. As our monarch, his power
was absolute.

When the day finally came, I found myself, gift in hand, on the
second floor of the Amsterdam Palace. There were many people
there, and I recognized only a handful: the king and queen; the
military secretary to the king; Dr. Halder, the personal physician
to the king; and the Nepalese Ambassador to Germany and
Netherlands, Sardar Bhim Bahadur Pandey. The ambassador
introduced me to the king.

"Your Majesty, Mr. Prabasi is a student at the Institute of
Social Studies here. He is the only Nepali in the Netherlands at
this time. I have known him for some months, and he is a credit
to our country."

I bowed down with folded hands as is customary in Nepal.

"How long have you been here?" the king asked me.

"Approximately two years, Your Majesty." I replied, still half-
bowed, showing appropriate deference.

"What do you plan to do next?"

"After completing the course, I'd like to do some more research in my field of development studies in this country."

"That sounds like a fine idea. If you need any help, you can send a petition for my consideration."

I smiled, and said, "Sarkar (Your Majesty), I do not know if my petition will reach you, as there are four gates to your palace."

He smiled back and looked at our Ambassador, "Bhim Bahadur, make sure that Satish Prabasi's letter comes via the south gate of the palace."

He looked back at me and said, "It will certainly reach me."

"What is your father's name?" he asked me suddenly.

I stood up straight. "Your Majesty would not know my father. I am not from a pedigreed family."

At this, his face clouded over, and there was a hush in the room, as if everyone was holding their breath.

The King gave me a long look. "Anyway, your father must have a name."

"Yes, Your Majesty, all the Nepalese have a name—some are just more prestigious. My father is Lekhnath Upadhyaya."

He looked at me again and said, "You certainly know how to hold a conversation. I am glad you are studying here. Nepal needs people like you."

He looked at the Ambassador and said, "Keep an eye out for him."

The room was suddenly warm and friendly again. I was still standing there when he asked me to sit down. I sat as per his command, but after five minutes or so, I asked for permission to go back to The Hague, where I had other duties.

The Nepalese ambassador walked me out, and in the corridor, he said sternly, "You almost ruined your career." The subtext of the ambassador's statement was that I could have made the king furious by saying that there were pedigreed families in Nepal. It was my good luck that the king ignored my observation.

In the summer months of July and August, the ISS was deserted, except for a couple members of the library staff, receptionists, and the rare faculty member who did not go on holiday. For my holidays, I went to West Germany. I spent quite a few weeks in Bonn in the spacious apartment of the first secretary of our embassy, Keshav Raj Jha. It was another uncertain time in my life. I had completed my course in the Netherlands, and I desperately wished to remain there to continue research or embark somehow on an academic career, but I had no immediate prospects for a job, and my summer vacation in Germany was over. I was returning to the Netherlands, where I still had my accommodation through the ISS, but I wasn't sure what I would be doing next.

Soon after I got back to The Hague, in the autumn of 1967, I got a call from Rector Jan Glastra van Loon's office to meet with him. Before his rectorship, he was a professor of European history and law at Leiden University. He was always charming, but even more so that day.

"What are your plans after completing your master's, Satish?"

"I'd love to remain in the Netherlands. I find this country and society much more tolerant and appreciative of different cultures than England or Germany, where I have spent some time. But I don't know how I can do it."

"I have a proposal," the rector replied. "How would you like to join our faculty and run the course that you have just completed?"

This was quite unexpected, like a gift from heaven. I immediately replied, "I would be grateful if you could employ me. But what would be my duties?"

"We have been impressed by your academic talent and also your ability to manage differences between students from different cultures and pave the way for friendships between them. You know that national development is an interdisciplinary course. My staff tell me you excelled in connecting the dots between economics, sociology, and politics. So, if you are interested, we will hire you from next month as you will have to prepare changes in the curricula and some additional books for reading, and you can get some experience under your belt. Then, as you know, the chairmanship of the course rotates, so, you will chair the course from the next academic year."

I was deeply excited by this unusual offer. In 1968, I accepted a position as a lecturer at the ISS to conduct the national development course. I had the pleasure of organizing field trips and study-abroad programs. Within a year of starting my new job, I was working on academic cooperation with UN specialized agencies such as the ILO, UNESCO, and UNICEF. This phase eventually led me to work in five African countries: Ethiopia, Kenya, Tanzania, Uganda, and Zambia. As it had at key moments throughout my life, my luck had come through again.

CHAPTER 18

IT'S A SMALL WORLD

THERE is a saying in South Asia that the reality on the ground looks different from two sides of the fence. As a student, I was familiar with the different groups and cliques that formed among the participants of the course. Now, as a lecturer, my experience of the group dynamics and interactions between students of different nationalities was quite different again.

The participants from India and Pakistan became acrimonious after the 1965 war. The perennial conflict caused by Kashmir, a mountainous kingdom in the Himalayas, kept festering and creating tensions between Indian and Pakistani colleagues at the Institute. I was well versed in Hindi, the language of India, and Urdu, the language of Pakistan. The students from these countries each expected me to take their side, which I was unwilling and unable to do.

We had a handful of participants from Israel, and a dozen or so from the Middle East—from Egypt, Jordan, and Iraq. After the Six Day War, these students no longer ate together at the student dining tables and stopped speaking with one another. The political and cultural issues back home began to be projected and amplified at the ISS.

I also remember a senior official of the government of India, who had come for a ten-month course in international relations. Mr. Bharadwaj came to me one afternoon to complain about a serious matter.

"Mr. Prabasi, I have a complaint, and I need your intervention."

"What is it Mr. Bharadwaj? How can I help you?"

"A derogatory film about India is being shown at the movie theater near the institute. It's called *The Party* by this fellow Peter Sellers. He imitates our accent and denigrates our culture."

"Well, Mr. Bharadwaj, it's a movie. One can either laugh at it or critique it, but you cannot prevent it from being shown."

He became tense and told me, "You are being anti-Indian as usual. I shall go and complain to our ambassador."

I was told later by my Indian colleagues that he did go to the embassy to complain and was roundly rebuked by the ambassador, who explained the concept of freedom of expression. I watched *The Party* and became a fan of Peter Sellers.

After thinking about these problems of incompatibility, I started a program of Friday afternoon seminars at the bar next to the ISS called Het Moulen. I would invite antagonistic groups of students to express their views or hypotheses in a civil and courteous manner. In the beginning, they were stiff, but after a couple of beers, along with the Dutch snack *bitterballen*, they would mellow down, and some constructive conversations could take place. Initially, I would pay for the first couple of rounds of beers, and gradually they would offer to pay the next round. My Friday afternoon seminars became quite popular and well attended.

CHAPTER 19

A NEW ARC OF HAPPINESS

Iwas deeply engaged in the management and conduct of my course when I received a letter from Bangkok. The stamp on the envelope read, "Royal Nepal Embassy, Thailand." I was intrigued as to who might be sending me a letter from there.

It was written by Devendra Raj Upadhya, then Chargé d'Affaires in Thailand, and his wife, Sarala Upadhya. It was the same family with whom I had stayed during my studies in Kathmandu. They were son and daughter-n-law of Subhadra sanima. All of them had been very helpful to me. In their letter, they proposed that I marry Jyotsna, who was Sarala's youngest sister. Jyotsna was the name her parents had given her, but when she started school, she became annoyed that so many people were mispronouncing her name. She chose a new name for herself, Sheila, and had her name legally changed. At home, she was still known as Jyotsna, but at school and elsewhere, she was Sheila. I had known Jyotsna as a secondary-school girl in Kathmandu. Her eldest brother was a colleague of mine, both in the Rapti Valley project and in Singha Durbar. Consequently, I was familiar with all the members of his family, including Jyotsna, from my visits to his home. I had also often met Sheila at her sister's house.

I still remember the young, beautiful girl who radiated innocence and joy at life. She was very good in sports, and sometimes her brother Bipin-ji and I used to go and see her compete in races. In Nepali society, you would not be expected to express your attraction to young girls and female relatives. In traditional South Asian society, it is inappropriate for a young man to express a liking—much less love—for a woman to her kin. It may emerge in a period of time, but Western-style dating is not tolerated. Mutual attraction can be expressed in many ways, but it always has to be within cultural boundaries of appropriateness.

Though I was inextricably attracted to Jyotsna, I would be tongue-tied and unable to express my feelings in person. I also realized that it was not a selfish love on my part. I knew she wanted to study medicine and become a doctor. Additionally, my household in Kathmandu had enough burdens, so I could not even think of getting married to anyone—let alone Jyotsna. The suicide of my nephew Niranjan had cast such a deep sense of melancholy and sorrow over my time in Kathmandu that I had made up my mind to get away from Nepal.

The letter from Bangkok placed me in an emotional and intellectual dilemma. I was delighted at the prospect of getting married to Jyotsna, the one and only girl I was attracted to, but my Western education and personal values made me a little annoyed, raising such questions in my mind as, "How can they be suggesting this? Have they talked to her? How does she feel about this?" My journeys in Israel, Britain, and now the Netherlands had confirmed my belief in mutual love and consent to marriage, something that was not expected in Nepal, where marriages were often arranged by relatives. The new academic program had just begun, so I had to devote my time as the chairman of the course to its smooth functioning, but the proposal contained in the letter kept interrupting, and playing through my heart and mind.

I therefore composed a careful reply to Mr. and Mrs. Upadhya asking if they had consulted Jyotsna. Had she agreed to the proposal? "Until and unless I get a clear response from her, that she is agreeable to this arranged marriage, I will not be able to reply," I told them.

After posting the letter, I felt a sense of relief, in that I felt they would ask her now if they had not done so earlier. Weeks turned into months; guest lecturers came to my course and went away to England, France, and Italy; I continued grading my students' papers, but the one letter that I expected every day to receive from either Thailand or Nepal did not come. I reached an emotional point where I said to myself, "*C'est la vie.*"

Occasionally I would go with my Brazilian and Kenyan friends, Nailton and Paul Awiti, to nightclubs and bars in Scheveningen. The bars would be full of young and beautiful girls, either with their boyfriends or just having a night out with their friends. I would be holding a glass of Scotch or brandy and suddenly, out of nowhere, the mental image of Jyotsna would flash before my eyes. I would be rattled by it and mutter "*godver-domme*" to myself.

CHAPTER 20

MOMENTOUS NEWS

Finally, I received a letter in the middle of November from Bangkok informing me that Jyotsna had agreed to marry me. The same week, my friend Bipin also sent a letter, this one from Kathmandu, conveying the good news. The letter from Bipin also mentioned that the astrologers in Kathmandu had identified an auspicious date for the wedding, December 12, 1969.

Everyone was eagerly looking forward to our wedding. I had to fulfill certain rituals and ceremonies prior to our marriage, so I was advised by my relatives to contact Jyotsna's sister in Bangkok.

I was thrilled. I was also perplexed about all the preparations and the logistical details to be attended to. I had less than a month to buy a diamond ring, book a plane ticket to Bangkok, and after a week in Bangkok, fly onward to Kathmandu. I shared my worries with Jan van Lochem. By this time, he and I had become close friends. My main worry was about how to get a visa to visit Bangkok, on the strength of a letter of recommendation from the

ISS. Jan was kind enough to write a letter in Dutch to the Thai embassy in support of my visa application, and he facilitated the process of a three-week leave of absence in the middle of the academic year to fly out, get married, and bring back my new bride.

The visit to Bangkok was problematic. I was given enough hints that I would have to buy gold jewelry; some gold items were essential for performing the wedding ceremony, and others were tokens of my love and respect. I had no idea what to buy, how many things to buy, or where in Bangkok I should go to buy them. Sarala bhauju helped me greatly in my shopping adventures, and I managed to buy the gold and ornate fabrics for saris I needed. I recall that the personnel of the Nepalese embassy in Thailand used to patronize a jewelry store owned by a man appropriately called Mr. Thip (A Thai word derived from the Sanskrit word Deep which means a lighted lamp).

I flew to Kathmandu with my Thai shopping, laden with more gold than I had ever held. Once again in my life, Subhadra sanima helped me, by arranging a place to stay in her house, finding the priest to conduct the wedding ceremony according to Hindu customs, and making other arrangements required for my marriage with Jyotsna.

I finally had returned to Kathmandu after five years, and I was astonished and shocked by several aspects of life that I had not noticed earlier—or to which I had not given enough attention. The beautiful city had grown filthier. Young children defecated on the open road, and rundown taxis and auto rickshaws cared neither for the rules of driving, nor for the hazard to pedestrians. Time management was an essential aspect of Dutch life to which I had grown accustomed. But in Kathmandu, there were only three times: morning, afternoon, and night. After our wedding, a group of musicians had to perform in the streets to take the new bride to her husband's abode; my musicians arrived two hours late, which made me so mad that I harangued them without realizing that I was making my newlywed bride terrified of her angry new husband.

The old priest who conducted the ceremony had mentioned that it would take twelve hours to complete the entire ceremony. I shuddered at the thought of those endless hours. I mentioned to him that I was a teacher in the Netherlands and that we had two kinds of books: the full version and the abridged version. Couldn't he perform an abridged version of the ceremony? Earlier, I had noticed that the priest was fascinated by my cell-operated transistor radio. I offered him my radio as a sign of my appreciation for his shortening the ceremony. He accepted and cut the process to about half the time. As an economist, I noted that Adam Smith's perception of market forces also applied to Hindu traditions.

We stayed in Kathmandu for twelve days, during which time various rituals and celebrations continued. As a new couple, Jyotsna and I were expected to pay our respects to a considerable number of people in both our extended families. In addition, we had to visit temples and holy places around Kathmandu to offer our prayers and receive blessings from an impressive array of gods and goddesses.

I had to return to the ISS before January 3, 1970, and on January 5, I had to deliver a lecture to my class that had been arranged long before my leave was granted. Sheila and I left Kathmandu for Delhi on December 24, I with a sense of joy and relief, and she with a heavy heart and teary eyes. We had a reservation at the Lodhi Hotel near the famed Lodhi Gardens. After our night in Delhi, we flew by Alitalia to Rome, and then onward to Amsterdam. After we got to Schiphol, we took a bus to The Hague.

I was very happy to return to The Hague with Sheila, but also somewhat worried about how she would adjust to the new realities she faced—the harsh winter and loneliness away from family and friends in Nepal. I knew that my job at the ISS would keep me away, and she would be alone for most of the day. We had arranged that we would call each other during my lunch hour. I knew she loved ice cream, preferably with coconut in it, so I used to make sure to take her out often. She marveled that people ate ice cream in such cold weather.

I have very happy memories of our first few months of growing love and getting used to living together. I had lived alone in Europe for the last five years. With Sheila's arrival, I saw my apartment and lifestyle for the first time through her eyes. She was not pleased. Soon I was made aware of such important tasks as emptying my green glass ashtray on a regular basis, putting my socks in the laundry hamper, and not smoking in bed. Above all—the importance of stocking our kitchen with the proper tools, pots, and pans.

Our delayed honeymoon took place in May, when I was required to go to Rome with my students. It was a memorable visit to Rome. Sheila and I were given a wonderful rooftop marble suite adjacent to Piazza Navona. As I was the group leader, I was addressed by the hotel staff as *il capo*. Sheila asked me what "*capo*" meant. I really didn't know how to translate this properly, so I said, "The head: Chief." We enjoyed our visit to Rome and traveled further to Capri, Pompeii, Naples, and other towns in southern Italy. The contrast between the affluent north and the poor south was startling. And it reminded me of the book *Christ Stopped at Eboli*.

I have fond memories of Rome as an ancient and historic city. Being together with Sheila has given me further fragments of happy memories. I remember her reaction to the marvelous buffet hall in the hotel where we stayed. There was extensive display of seafood, including mussels, which I love very much.

When she saw me eating mussels, Sheila was horrified, and spoke aloud in Nepali language, "*Chhya, chhya, chhya....* you eat these types of dirty creatures?!" Her level of discomfort further increased when she saw a waiter bringing a large bottle of Chianti to our table. My food habits of eating mussels and drinking red wine at lunchtime almost spoiled her appetite altogether.

During our trip south, we rented a bus in Naples to go and meet senior officials of the regional development fund for southern Italy. In Bari, an attractive tourist spot, we disembarked from the bus. Small children, who were perhaps on a school break, saw Sheila and started chanting, "*La princessa, la princessa!*" Sheila always had a remarkable sense of fashion. In Bari she was dressed in a French chiffon sari that had brought the admiration of the children; they followed us for almost a mile until I had to finally confess that she was really a princess from a distant mountain kingdom. They clapped, some smiling and some laughing.

My young wife was smart and curious. When we visited an olive-pressing factory, she was fascinated to watch and ask questions about how the freshly pressed oil would be bottled and where it would be distributed. She was also very attentive during our visit to the Martini plant.

On our way back from our Italian journey, we stopped in Heidelberg to explore the town and hear a lecture about the city from a university professor. In the evening, when we boarded the train again, all the students and I ordered an evening dinner from the railway diner. I ordered a bottle of light and sweet German wine, Moselle.

Sheila asked me, "What are you drinking, my dear?"

I had a mischievous twinkle in my eye when I responded, "Try it; it's sweet and not too strong." She was thirsty, I think. So she sipped the wine, and after a minute or so, she drank the full glass as though it were juice.

I watched her closely, and in half an hour or so, "What was in that drink? I think there might have been some alcohol in it!" That was her first introduction to white wine, which she still loves.

The next year, I went with Sheila to spend the Christmas holidays in London at the invitation of Hans Ollman. Hans and his wife Catherine were gracious hosts and made us feel very comfortable. Catherine became a friend of Sheila's. Sheila was intrigued by the process of making Christmas pudding and other British holiday dishes. At night, when we went to the guest room, Sheila flatly refused to get into bed under an electric blanket. She was terrified that it would electrocute us in the middle of the night while we slept. I had to talk to Catherine to explain this situation, and she eventually reassured Sheila and persuaded her that the electric blanket was harmless.

One morning during our London holiday, we went sightseeing to the usual tourist places: Buckingham Palace, Oxford Street, Hyde Park, and others. Sheila seemed to be a little disappointed with the city. She said, "Why do they keep praising London? It is not that different from Calcutta." I explained to her that the architecture and public parks in Calcutta were modeled after London's. I had to admire her perception, though.

After our return to The Hague, I invited an Indian friend, Dev Bhalla, to dinner at our apartment. Dev had some reservations about the food that a young, newly arrived Nepali woman would prepare. He confided to me later on that before coming to dinner, he had eaten a heavy snack just in case.

When he tasted the meal prepared by Sheila, he was astonished. He asked, "Where did you learn to cook so well, Sheila?"

She replied with a confident smile, "I learned from my mom, who is the best cook in the world."

Upon hearing this, Dev replied, "Next time, I will bring Ida." Ida was his girlfriend, though Dev was also married and had a young daughter of whom I was very fond.

I suggested that Ida might teach Sheila some Dutch and help her learn about Dutch culture to help her adjust to life in the Netherlands.

Ida was a schoolteacher who had days off on Wednesdays. She agreed to meet with Sheila mid-week, which was a big relief for me, since I would be at the ISS. At that time, none of us would have guessed what a deep and strong bond Ida and Sheila would form; it has continued for more than four decades and is still going strong.

In 1970, Czech Republic and Slovakia were one country called Czechoslovakia. By all economic and social indicators, the European institutes of research and development including

OECD (Organization for Economic Cooperation and Development) indicated that Slovakia was a much poorer part of the country, similar to the situation in northern and southern Italy. During my earlier studies in the U.K., I had become aware of the disparity in development between northern and southern Italy. When the Czech Republic and Slovakia were amalgamated into Czechoslovakia, the prosperous and enlightened Czech region was far more advanced than Slovakia. I initiated a research program of comparing economic planning in a capitalist economy, that is, Italy, with planning in the Slovak region of Czechoslovakia.

Although Prague Spring, a period of liberalization under Communism, was headed by Alexander Dubcek, who was a Slovak, many complained that Slovakia was treated unfairly. Some people even considered the amalgamation an unjust exploitation of Slovakia by the Czech leadership. My research program, initiated in 1968 and continuing until 1970, was quite popular in that it allowed participants to visit Southern Italy as well as Slovakia.

CHAPTER 21

AFRICAN VISTA

IN the spring of 1970, Professor Jan Ponseion, the head of educational projects at the ISS, asked me if I would be interested in writing a research paper on educational innovations in Africa. He mentioned that it would involve a month of intensive study and comparative research followed by ten days of a seminar in Addis Ababa, Ethiopia. The project was funded by UNESCO and the Economic Commission for Africa (ECA), then headed by Mr. Gardiner, a distinguished Ghanaian.

I gladly accepted the offer. In addition to the interesting research and the opportunity to travel to Ethiopia, the work also offered a grant of $1,000 in U.S dollars. Having just come back from a wedding in Nepal involving considerable expenses, this amount was doubly attractive to me. Sheila helped me in writing the research paper by taking notes at night. She has legible and beautiful handwriting, something that cannot be said of my own. Her notes were typed out and made into a presentable document by my Dutch secretary, Jenny van der Meijle. In late April 1970, at the age of 30, I had the pleasure of visiting Ethiopia, my first experience on the African continent. I had read and heard about the Lion of Africa, His Imperial Majesty Haile Selassie, who was revered by many African leaders for his role in expelling the Italian fascists from his kingdom.

In those days there was no direct flight to Ethiopia so we boarded a KLM flight to Rome, and from there, we flew to Addis Ababa. When we disembarked, we went to the Ras Hotel, where the ECA had reserved hotel rooms for us. On our way to the hotel, I was overwhelmed with an aroma so delightful and invigorating that I asked the taxi driver about its source. He said, "Sir, the whole valley is surrounded by eucalyptus trees. In the morning, you should take a walk, and you will get the true aroma."

The next morning, after a quick breakfast, Professor Ponseion and I started a leisurely walk to the ECA building. The gentleman at the hotel's reception desk had warned us to be careful of the altitude of the city. He even gave us a few pills to take before going for our walk. However, both of us felt so happy and energetic that we put the pills in our pockets and continued our walk. After about half an hour, I suddenly saw a strange spectacle. A black Mercedes drove by slowly with the right-hand passenger window down. A young lion cub peered out of the window as I had seen puppies doing in the Netherlands. I didn't see anyone other than the driver, but the Ethiopians on the street bowed down, lying prostrate on the side of the road. We were told later by our hosts at the ECA that whenever the Emperor drove around the city, the people expressed their respect by bowing, almost lying down on the ground. They also told us that if we saw the lion cub, it meant that the emperor was inside the car; the cub was his pet animal.

While we were at the ECA, the building suddenly lost power, and the elevator did not work. We were told to wait in the lobby. The old Dutch professor suggested that we take the stairs up. The gentleman at the reception counter looked aghast at the prospect of the old man's walking so many stairs. He insisted, "No, sir; no, sir, you should not take the stairs."

Professor Ponseion insisted, "I'm healthy, and Mr. Prabasi is even healthier!"

We had hardly walked up two flights of stairs when suddenly Professor Ponseion collapsed. I panicked and ran down to the reception counter to get help. The receptionist came up with me, muttering, "I told you, sirs, not to do this." When we got to the professor, he was conscious, and the receptionist took him to the ECA health center where he could rest and recover. The professor was fine after a few hours; he was merely feeling the effects of the altitude.

I really enjoyed my first interaction with the African delegations at the ECA. They were well dressed in formal suits and ties or in colorful national dress, and they were extremely articulate and well spoken. I remember being taken aback by the exuberance of the laughter, joking, and backslapping among the delegates who knew each other. This was quite unusual from a Nepalese perspective.

Mr. Gardiner presented an eloquent paper on the problems of education and the need for innovation in education in the African continent. He was tall and patrician in appearance. For the next ten days, we enjoyed intellectual discussions and unique Ethiopian cuisine. For the first time in my life, I saw people being fed *injera*, the traditional soft, sour bread, by the hosts. There were cocktails every evening, but to Professor Ponseion's regret, he was advised not to drink. Happily, I had no such restrictions.

One Sunday, all delegates were driven by car to natural hot springs just outside the city. Filwoha, as it was called, was again a unique experience. When the seminar concluded, one of its recommendations was to request future UNESCO funding for the establishment of a university in Zambia. It was further suggested that faculty members from the University of Tanzania and Makerere University in Uganda should be involved in this initiative. This opened up the prospect of the ISS's getting involved in this ambitious project with the support of the Dutch Development

Fund. To my great delight, it also created an opportunity for me to continue my participation with ECA, UNESCO, and Dutch projects in East Africa.

Thanks to the initiative, I was able to visit Tanzania, Kenya, Uganda, and Zambia. It also gave me an opportunity to get involved in Africa's educational-development projects over a period of four years, when I made regular visits to these countries.

Tanzania was known in those days as the center of educational innovation at both the middle-school and higher-education levels. The University of Tanzania at Dar es Salaam was highly praised by international agencies like the World Bank and UNESCO. President Julius Nyerere had built a movement of self-reliance and inclusive development. Professors from the University of California and the Institute of Development Studies, headed by Dudley Sears, were also associated with the university.

My personal impressions were of a country led by a visionary leader trying to follow its own path of inclusive development. The civil servants were frank about the deficiencies of their own system, yet they remained quite confident of leading a new way. I was deeply touched by the concept of *Ujamaa*, the conception of extended community and collectivism developed by Julius Nyerere, which I saw being implemented during my visit to Tanzania.

I remember Uganda as a beautiful country noted for 'the Moon Mountain'. The capital city is Kampala, on the shores of Lake Victoria. My first arrival to the country was one that I would never forget. I had boarded East African Airways from Nairobi, Kenya, to Entebbe Airport in Uganda. When we landed at the airport, we were requested by the crew to remain seated until further announcements. The plane was full, and some of us had imbibed the generous free alcohol available on the flight. A group of young soldiers who looked like teenagers boarded the plane and gruffly started asking each passenger, "Are you an American?"

When my turn came, they asked me the same question. Being quite relaxed after a couple of in-flight drinks, I replied flippantly, "Do I look like an American?" The young soldier angrily replied, "Don't joke with me! Show me your passport!" I showed him my Nepalese passport, with the flag on the cover. Our flag is unusual: it is the only non-rectangular national flag in the world.

The boy-soldier took one look at my passport and said, "Why did you tear the flag?" He thought that I had defaced the flag. He turned the passport up and down. When his superior came and examined it, the soldiers eventually returned it to me. After one hour of questioning the passengers, we saw three Caucasian women taken off the plane. After this, the captain announced that we could now disembark. He also mentioned that a few passengers had been taken off the flight for further questioning.

Later I would learn that this was the day of the military coup by Idi Amin, and those three women who were taken off our plane were from Israel. We later read in the papers in Zambia that the women had been killed.

By the time I visited Kampala again, the situation had deteriorated drastically. Idi Amin had an anti-intellectual streak, and we were told of his fascination with young women. I was told during my second visit by some of my trusted colleagues at the university that many young female students from the nursing school were abducted, raped, and killed. Consequently, the nursing school had been almost abandoned. I also heard that some of the radical professors at Makerere University, one of the finest institutions on the continent in those days, had disappeared. After a few days, their bodies were found floating in Lake Victoria.

Because of this torturous history, many faculty members from Makerere University had moved to Western Europe or to universities in the United States, including our principal contact, Professor Marzue. It was so sad to see such an outstanding institution destroyed by the ruler of the country.

Before going to Lusaka, I had experience of four African capital cities, the regal Addis Ababa, very much influenced by Italian architecture and cuisine; Nairobi, a colonial city built up by the British; Kampala, the capital city of Uganda; and Dar es Salaam. Each of these cities had their own characteristics. Addis Ababa had a unique blend of old and new palaces and white Italian-style palazzos, together with buildings that housed modern institutions such as Economic Commission for Africa, the headquarter of Organization of African Unity (OAU) etc.

Nairobi, the capital of Kenya, had a distinct flavor of a colonial city in those days. While the lovely parks there reminded one of English gardens, the neighborhoods were somewhat crammed with unemployed Kenyans. The lifestyle of well-to-do Kenyans was similar to the British middle class, and the ghettos were full of urban squalor. There for the first time in my life I saw that many buildings prominently displayed 'No Vacancy' signs. My friends told me that it was a sign to avoid thieves and gangsters from breaking in to the house.

Kampala, a quiet city on the shores of Lake Victoria, was the intellectual capital of East Africa before the military coup d'état by Idi Amin. Dar es Salaam, on the other hand, reflected a personality of the then-President of Tanzania, Julius Nyerere. It was a semi-rural, semi-urban city with a focus on austerity. President Nyerere was known as 'teacher' in the Swahili language because he tried to inculcate moral values among the population. He also started a somewhat revolutionary movement called Ujamaa Village Program. Zambia, which was earlier known as Northern Rhodesia, was a vast expanse of unending bushes and grasslands. There were attempts at urban planning, but the scale of the problem was so great that investment in urban development was a dream rather than a doable plan.

I visited Lusaka, the capital of Zambia, three times over a period of four years. My impression during the first visit was that of a sleepy town which would never grow into a metropolis. There were miles and miles of savannah grass around the town. People would indicate by pointing to the east, west, and other directions, and say proudly that a certain location will house in future the grand government secretariat, new hotels such as the Hilton, and the commercial plaza. It was hard to imagine. These were maize-growing areas where I could not imagine private investment for urban development.

There was only one small hotel, called Hotel Ridgeway, where tourists and visitors would stay, and local bigwigs would assemble in the evening for beer, liquor, and dancing. Most of the expats had to book rooms in advance. This is where I was introduced to a popular local snack called "chicken in the basket." I was well received by the Zambian officials, especially from the Ministry of Education and Culture. I was told that Nepal's late king Mahendra had participated in the meeting of non-aligned countries hosted by Zambia. King Mahendra's insistence on nationalism, and his flair for and skill as a hunter, had made him a memorable personality among the Zambians.

During my final visit to the city in 1974, the highways and lanes had been delineated, some of them even built up—especially the road connecting the international airport to the town. The University of Lusaka had many donors and foreign visitors at the time. There were Yugoslav professors, Cuban doctors, Swiss mathematicians, and academics from countless other countries. I remember that out of 82 faculty members, only the chancellor was a Zambian national. It was a chaotic situation that made us despair for the university and the country's development.

The country, which had been called Northern Rhodesia only a few years before, had a devout Christian president named Kenneth Kaunda, who was known to burst into tears and weep profusely in public meetings about his country's prospects. But he would accept all kinds of gifts and donations without any prioritization or strategy. My Dutch friend from NUFFIC (The Dutch organization for internationalization in education) and I stayed for two months during our last visit to Lusaka. I missed the Netherlands; realistically speaking, we thought the university wouldn't come into its own for another twenty years. So we wrote our final report, containing our blunt assessment of the bleak prospects for higher education in Zambia, and submitted it to the Dutch government and UNESCO.

I was keen to return to The Hague for another reason. Sheila had been pregnant for four months when I left for Zambia. Now, she was in her sixth month of pregnancy, and I was eager to get back.

CHAPTER 22

BECOMING PARENTS

IT was a pure joy to come back to the Netherlands after my trip to Zambia. Reuniting with Sheila after such a long separation was a relief and a delight. I felt guilty for leaving her alone while she was coping with her first pregnancy. I was told that Ida had been a great help to her, as had my friend Dev Bhalla. Bhalla had insisted that Sheila stay with him and his family while I was away. His girlfriend, the great romantic love of his life, had been accompanying Sheila during her appointments and generally supporting her as her closest female friend in the Netherlands. It was a delicate situation by any measure. But somehow, Sheila's exceptional social skills and diplomacy contributed to a peaceful coexistence.

Sheila and I were going to be parents in the Netherlands, where we had no family members. We had no knowledge nor guidance for the birth of a child. We had decided that our child should have a spacious environment with a little garden where the little one could appreciate the beauty of nature. Sheila's brother, Saroj Sharma, who had then come to the Netherlands from Germany, accompanied me in house hunting with the aid of Sunday newspapers. As luck would have it, during our last taxi ride, we found a newly built lovely house, close to the Hook of Holland (a busy shipping channel between the Netherlands and the U.K). It was somewhat expensive, but my heart was sold on it.

Our regular visits to Sheila's doctor, a gynecologist of Czech origin, led to my friendship with him. "Satish and Sheila, you must choose two names—one for a boy, and one for a girl. As soon as the child is born, we must inform the municipality with the details of the birth, including the name."

Sheila and I exchanged an uncomfortable glance. In our culture, it is inauspicious to name a child before its birth. In fact, we have a religious ceremony to name the child six days after birth. There are pragmatic reasons for this custom, too, since many newborns in South Asia do not survive their first few days of life. Choosing names at this time seemed rash, but the doctor was insistent.

"You are in the Netherlands now, and this is how it is done here. So please have your two names ready."

During our next visit, I told the doctor, "Okay, doctor, we have one name now. It is a girl's name: Sarina."

"And what about a boy's name?"

"It will not be a boy," I replied confidently, "so we don't need to pick a boy's name."

The doctor was taken aback. "But what if it is a boy?"

"It will not be," I insisted.

"Okay, then, Mr. Prabasi. If you are sure, let's have a wager. If it's a girl, you win, and I will give you a bottle of sherry. If it is a boy, the bottle of sherry is on you."

We shook hands on the bet, both smiling. Sheila was smiling too. "Doctor, Satish will always wager on a bottle."

Sheila was due on February 1st, and was admitted to the hospital a few days later; still, the baby did not come. After a week had passed, the doctors were ready to induce her labor and told her that if nothing happened naturally, they would intervene. That evening, her labor started, and our baby was born ten minutes after midnight.

The doctor beamed at me and said, "Satish, I lost our bet." I was delighted that Sarina had arrived, and I had won the bet. I was keen to have a girl child because I firmly believed, then and now, that girls are the basis of human progress. Our family deity in Nepal is the goddess Kali, who is the destroyer of evil and promoter of human welfare. Moreover, during my close study of India, I had been struck by the fact that while Mahatma Gandhi had four sons, very few people remembered their names. Jawaharlal Nehru had only one daughter, and the whole world knew her as Indira Gandhi. To me, the Asian preference for a male child was an obstacle to social progress. From a young age, I had a firm belief that progress in South Asian societies would only come with the advancement of women. I was determined to counter the prevailing discrimination against women and girls in my personal and professional life.

It was a cold February morning with crisp air and frozen snow all over the driveway of Star of Bethlehem Hospital. After eleven days of forced stay in the hospital (due to the late delivery of the baby), Sheila was eager to return home. I was also keen to bring her back.

I had arranged with a family friend to pick us up from the hospital. The pediatric nurse of the municipality where we lived had given me a long list of things to buy for the mother and the newborn. I had accordingly bought the pram, baby blankets, milk bottles, nappies, etc. This list helped us a lot. Yet, as new parents we were anxious to make no mistake in the care of the new baby. So as an insurance on my part I had bought, and read a couple of times, the best book on child care in those days, Dr. Benjamin Spock's *Baby and Child Care*. In fact, the book became my guide book. Sheila and I had no female relatives in the Netherlands to advise us on how to look after the young one. So, we were really concerned not to make any mistakes. Our next-door Dutch neighbor who had two young children helped us in the beginning. Similarly, the municipal nurse went out of her way to help and cheer up Sheila.

The arrival of the new baby in the Prabasi family created new sources of happiness as well as anxieties. I was extremely worried even in holding my young daughter lest I press her tender bones too hard. The new habit of waking up in the middle of the night to monitor the sleeping position of the young one, as well as her mother, was another new chore added to my list of things to do.

I knew that a month after the birth of Sarina, I was scheduled to go to Bangkok on a six-month assignment with the United Nations Economic and Social Commission for Asia and the Pacific (ESCAP). I asked our nurse if the mother and the baby could travel with me. She flatly refused to allow the young baby to travel before she was ten weeks old. Hence, I was again mentally disturbed at leaving my dearest ones in the Netherlands. As usual, Sheila encouraged me to go. She convinced me that she would be ok, especially with the help of our friend Ida and Dr. Bhalla's family. Moreover, her brother Mr. Sharma was also there.

Sheila and Sarina came to Bangkok in the month of April, after mandatory inoculations were completed. I still remember the blazing sun and the consequent heat at Don Mueang International Airport when I went to receive them from the Netherlands on a KLM Dutch airline flight. Sarina was wrapped in a soft woolen blanket. The young baby began to cry immediately after the plane touched the ground. It was Sarina's first exposure to the tropical heat of South East Asia.

After the airport formalities were over, we took an air-conditioned taxi to my apartment at Sukhumvit Road. Sarina grew in Bangkok from a baby to a toddler, and both Sheila and I had new sources of pleasure as well as worries. We were happy to watch the toothless smile of a toddler, but also worried that she might crush her fingers at the door of the apartment. Nevertheless, the six months spent in Bangkok were idyllic to both of us.

CHAPTER 23

GOODBYES

MY work at the Institute of Social Studies gave me my first exposure to, and opportunities with, the United Nations and its specialized agencies. I have mentioned earlier the ECA and UNESCO; now, I received a short-term contract with the Economic and Social Commission for Asia and the Pacific (ESCAP). Under the academic exchange program between ISS and the United Nations University in Japan, I had a chance to work for six months with the Asian Institute of Development and Planning in Bangkok, then located at Authya Road.

One year after returning to The Hague, I received a preliminary inquiry from UNICEF, in New York. They wanted to know if I was interested in working with them on a longer-term basis, with the prospect of permanent employment. They had job openings in Bangkok, New Delhi, and Jakarta.

After discussing with Sheila the pros and cons of moving to Asia from our settled situation in the Netherlands, we opted for New Delhi, where I accepted the role of regional planning officer for south-central Asia. The position involved developing policies for children's and women's welfare in seven countries in the region: Afghanistan, Bhutan, India, the Maldives, Nepal, Sri Lanka, and Mongolia. I found it somewhat odd that Mongolia, a country located in northeast Asia, was grouped with India and Afghanistan. Later, I came to learn that Pakistan had adamantly and absolutely refused to be part of a grouping with India. Hence, in typical UN style, Pakistan was grouped with countries in West Asia, while Mongolia was added to the South Asian group.

After some administrative negotiations, UNICEF asked me to visit the office in New Delhi for a week on an orientation visit. There, I met the director of the office, Mr. John Gruen, a Dutch national, and my predecessor, Victor Soler. Among my many reminiscences of that visit, I remember two major things: first, UNICEF India had programs for cooperating with twelve ministries and departments, almost mirroring the pattern of British administration. Secondly, I recall Mr. Gruen's remarks during a cordial lunch he had arranged at his home. In response to my general query as to how he liked being in New Delhi, he replied, "Mr. Prabasi, this place is so crowded and full of noise. You cannot go for a picnic lunch to Lodhi Park. As soon as you open your picnic box, a sizable number of strangers begin to stare at you. In addition, a hoard of stray dogs would encircle you. There is no privacy, nor quiet in this place."

Startled, I thought to myself, "This gentleman is thoroughly unhappy here. How does he interact with Indian officials?" To be generous to Gruen, I thought to myself, "Maybe this is the young gin speaking." He had been drinking during lunch.

I informed the Rector of the Institute of Social Studies upon my return from New Delhi that I wished to apply for long-term leave without pay because I would be working with UNICEF in India. He reluctantly agreed. Sheila and I then began packing, putting the house up for rent, arranging with our bank the payment of our taxes, and more. This would be the first of our many moves together aided by Sheila's careful planning, coordination, and execution.

During this period of transition, I felt sentimental. I initiated my goodbyes to friends and colleagues, starting with Jan Tinbergen, my friend and mentor. I began visiting the Mauritshuis Museum in The Hague to see the paintings of Vermeer, and the Rijksmuseum and the Van Gogh Museum in Amsterdam, as part of my emotional farewells.

I had been fond of the Dutch painter Vincent van Gogh because his own paintings had been influenced by what was known as *Japonisme* in nineteenth-century Europe. I re-read van Gogh's letters to his brother Theo. In one of his letters from Japan, he wrote, "I'd like you to spend some time here, you'd feel it—after some time your vision changes, you see with a more Japanese eye, you feel color differently."

CHAPTER 24

NEW DELHI

S HEILA, Sarina, and I boarded the KLM flight to New Delhi on August 17th, 1975. Thus began a family journey to a career in different lands. Being a Nepalese national, from a country squeezed between the two giants of China to the north and India to the south, I was fascinated by the divergent paths taken by Nepal's neighbors. While leaving the Netherlands for India, I had a deeply hidden wish in my heart to spend some time in China, too. I had not shared this dream even with Sheila.

1975 was not an auspicious time to be in India. The democratic fabric of the Indian government, so carefully nurtured by India's first prime minister, was rudely shaken by his own daughter. She imposed a state of emergency, an authoritarian system of rule that lasted for twenty-two months. Indira Gandhi and her younger son, Sanjay, ruled India as their personal fiefdom. Thousands of their political opponents, including members of parliament, were imprisoned. The press was censored. There was an air of palpable fear. Even the street vendors, reliably voluble in their opinions, would not discuss current events and the news. The government's decision-making process had been subverted by the mother-and-son team. In this climate of fear, one sycophant of Indira Gandhi, the leader of Gandhi's Indian National Congress, Dev Kant Barooah, declared, "India is Indira. Indira is India."

One morning, Mr. Gruen phoned me to meet him in his office. "Satish, there is a high-brow intellectual coming to my office at 11:00 am. Can you come and talk to him, and keep him company, and find out what he wants?"

I went to Mr. Gruen's office and met a tall and handsome American with an intense look about him. He introduced himself.

"Jim Grant, with the Overseas Development Council in Washington, D.C. I'm working now on the PQLI index—that is, the Physical Quality of Life Index." Mr. Gruen said hurriedly, "Mr. Grant, I have a couple of appointments this morning, so our planning officer, Satish, whom you just met, will explain to you the work we do." He then glanced at his ever-elegant secretary. "Indira, can you please arrange for coffee and some snacks in Satish's office?" He got up from his chair, shook hands with Mr. Grant, and told me in his gruff voice, "You're in charge."

I was a little perplexed by the brusque behavior of my boss. Mr. Grant and I walked to my office, which was in the adjacent building. Soon after we started talking, it was clear that Mr. Grant and I had a rapport; we "clicked" during our discussion. He told me about his background and earlier work with USAID in Southeast Asia. He then gave me a detailed presentation on the PQLI and how, in his opinion, Sri Lanka and the state of Kerala in India had developed much faster than the national average.

Talking with Mr. Grant was an intellectual tonic for me. After some months in a bureaucratic work culture, I was thrilled to meet someone like Jim Grant, with whom I could have a "high-brow" dialogue, to borrow Mr. Gruen's phrase.

We were soon on a first-name basis, and Jim asked me if I knew a Professor K. N. Raj, who was then the chair of the Institute of Development Studies at Trivandrum in Kerala. I mentioned that Professor Raj was in New Delhi for discussions with the then-Planning Commission about resource allocation to the state of Kerala. Mr. Grant became very animated and asked if I could put him in contact with Professor Raj. I laughed and said I would do it gladly if he would join me for lunch at the Claridges Hotel. We went for lunch, and I called my friend Krishna Murthy in the Social Development Division of the Planning Commission. While Mr. Grant and I were still having lunch, Krishna Murthy called me back with the local contact number for the professor. Jim was delighted. He told me that the professor was an old friend. He would arrange to meet with him before flying out to Colombo via Chennai. He told me that he would be in Madras for two days to attend the opening ceremony of the Pugwash International Conference against Nuclear Armament.

When I bid him goodbye in the lobby of the hotel, Jim looked at me intently. "I am glad you are working with UNICEF here. I feel we will meet again as I keep passing through India."

I smiled and replied, "Who knows?" I did not know then that Jim's father, John Black Grant, had worked in Calcutta, nor that a medical institute for the treatment of tropical diseases was named after him.

It was the custom in UNICEF India to report to the regional director the gist of meetings and professional discussions, including things I felt were of a trivial or secondary nature. If the subject matter was of major concern, then one had to submit a formal written report. In keeping with this tradition, I went to Mr. Gruen during the late afternoon that day and informed him of my meeting with Mr. Grant, including lunch.

"Thank you, Satish, for taking care of Mr. Grant. Who paid for the lunch?"

I thought this was a very Dutch question and replied, "I did, from my own wallet." I smiled. "John, I am paid enough by UNICEF to host colleagues and friends occasionally."

"How long will he stay in India?"

"I understand he is flying to Madras to attend the Pugwash conference to be inaugurated by Mrs. Indira Gandhi."

Gruen exclaimed, "Oh, that reminds me! We have also received an invitation to attend the conference. I don't think I will go. Would you like to go, Satish?"

I beamed and replied, "I will be happy to go if you think it is appropriate."

He asked his secretary Indira to send his files to my office. Thus, a disdainful Dutch director enabled me to meet and shake hands with Mrs. Gandhi. It was also a chance to meet world-renowned scientists and thinkers. The conference was to be held at Hotel Connemara. I spent four days there participating in discussions on different aspects of the nuclear menace.

I started to feel unhappy with the style of work at UNICEF. It brought back my memories of Nepalese bureaucracy, where files moved, but the eyes and vision were blinkered. My contacts in the Indian government indicated their unhappiness with the leadership of John Gruen. Local staff spread throughout the state capitals and in New Delhi had begun to be vocally against international staff. I spoke Hindi well and understood the ethos of my Indian colleagues, so they opened up to me candidly. They encouraged me to talk to Gruen about these matters. But being new to the organization, with less than one year of service under my belt, I knew I was not in a position to do so.

My relationship with the regional director was complex. He trusted and shared his innermost thoughts with me. Since I had come from the Netherlands and knew the Dutch people and their ways, he was comfortable with me. John came from Leiden, a university town with over 700 years of academic and cultural history. We would often reminisce about the city. Nonetheless I found myself in a quandary about my options to address the deteriorating and sterile work environment.

My visit to Bhutan was a second great experience during this time. John Gruen liked this small Buddhist country, tucked in the high Himalayas between India and China. UNICEF operations in Bhutan had been managed by our Nepal office in the past, but after Indira Gandhi declared the state of emergency, visits to Bhutan were made extremely difficult by the Indian authorities. As regional director, John was granted permission by the Ministry of External Affairs to travel to the sensitive northeast border of India and to cross the border into Bhutan.

In December 1976, John arranged to visit Thimphu, the capital city of Bhutan. He asked me to join him. I was very pleased and felt grateful to John for including me. Our office arranged our visas and other administrative details. We flew to Calcutta. After seven hours at the airport, we took a flight to Bagdogra, the military airport in Assam. The Ministry of Foreign Affairs in Bhutan arranged to send a vehicle to the Indian airport to drive us to Thimphu. We reached Phuntsholing, the border town, late in the evening. We retired for the night and started our picturesque mountain drive in the morning.

I was captivated beyond my imagination by the beautiful range of mountains and densely populated flowering forests along the way. Although I had seen Nepalese mountains and a wide variety of beautiful plants, I had never seen such magical scenery. Buddhist prayer flags fluttered in every valley, and the melodious sounds of small bells tied to the necks of cattle and yaks reminded me of the Swiss countryside. We reached Thimphu in the late afternoon and rested in the government guesthouse.

The Ministry of Foreign Affairs had arranged a lavish dinner in honor of Mr. Gruen. I remember the foreign minister Dawa Tsering, graced the occasion, and to my great surprise, he spoke to me in fluent Nepali. Apparently, the Bhutanese embassy in New Delhi had shared my résumé with the government. The next morning, we had productive discussions on our cooperative program on health and education in the Central Secretariat. On the third day, we drove to the beautiful Paro Valley. We visited the National Museum of Bhutan for a couple of hours, and we were taken to a nurses' training school being built with UNICEF assistance.

Although John declined the climb to visit a century-old monastery, I did go with a guide, and had a deeply educational experience about historical aspects of Bhutanese Buddhism. On the fourth day, we returned to Thimphu and had another round of discussions with various ministries and departments. Mr. Gruen spoke with Chief Secretary Dasho Tobgyel.

"From now on, Satish Prabasi will be looking after the Bhutan program from the UNICEF office, New Delhi. It will be difficult for Americans and Europeans to get entry visas to Bhutan via the government of India. So I've decided to hand over the responsibilities of program development in Bhutan to Mr. Prabasi. I have not told him this yet, but I will brief him on our return journey. I can assure you, Dasho, that the program will be in capable hands."

Everyone looked delighted in the conference room, and I was stunned.

I had the privilege and pleasure of working for six years in South Asia for the benefit of children and women. During this period, I visited Bhutan every six months. This worked well for the government and me to review progress, solve problems, and set new directions. I remember that the king of Bhutan granted me an audience in his private chambers during one of my visits. As a token of appreciation, he bestowed on me a *khata* (a traditional ceremonial white scarf), a beautiful *thangka* painting, and a pair of exquisitely carved and colorful Bhutanese folding tables.

On another occasion, as I traveled with my family, I had the unexpected pleasure of meeting Tenzing Norgay, the mountaineer who climbed Mount Everest with Sir Edmund Hillary. He and his party were traveling and climbing in Bhutan. My daughter, Sarina, had the presence of mind to ask for and obtain his autograph.

A third major event occurred a week after John and I returned from our visit to Bhutan. We were happy and energized; I was excited by the prospect of being given responsibility for the Bhutan program. But my contacts in the Indian government hinted to me that the Prime Minister's office was considering sending a discreet request to replace John as the director of UNICEF India. It would not be a formal request, but they were adamant that this should be done. I was deeply disturbed. Our local UNICEF staff seemed to be more cheerful than when I had left them, so perhaps they were aware of the situation, too. I did not know what to do.

CHAPTER 25

OFFICE POLITICS: LEARNING THE ROPES

O NE evening, I received a call from New York instructing me to check my faxes in the office. I returned to my office in Jor Bagh, a neighborhood in New Delhi, late in the evening and found a detailed fax message from our deputy executive director, Mr. Dick Heyward. An Australian by birth and a statistician by training, Mr. Heyward was a legend in UNICEF. He was a workaholic who did not like to hang around the cocktail crowd of the UN. He asked me to do two things: prepare a concise and clear note on the current situation in the UNICEF regional office, including a few paragraphs about my perspective on possible areas of improvement. This note must be strictly private and personal. Secondly, I was instructed not to plan any travel until Mr. Hayward's upcoming visit to New Delhi for a week. I acknowledged the fax and informed our headquarters that my note would be ready. The fax was marked, "for your eyes only."

The next two weeks were most miserable for me. I could share neither the news that Mr. Hayward was on the way to India, nor my delicate task of preparing the assessment. We did not have a computer in our office, so I had to devise a secure and discreet way to write the assessment. My personal assistant used to come to my residence sometimes to take notes in the evenings. He was discreet and dependable. My note was prepared in absolute privacy without any possibility of leaks.

Events moved quickly in the latter half of his visit. Mr. Hayward asked me directly during our lunch meeting, "Satish, do you think it would help if we were to transfer John?"

"That is not for me to say, sir. I do believe that our regional office should be headed by someone who knows India and has empathy for its people."

After some more pleasantries, he asked, "Do you know Mr. Davies?"

"No, sir, I do not."

"Mr. Davies has been UNICEF's regional director in India in the past. He's a Quaker and married to a Bengali woman, a distant relative of Rabindranath Tagore, the Bengali poet who received the Nobel Prize for literature."

My face must have given me away at the possibility of working with Davies, though I said nothing. Mr. Hayward looked at me and said, "So, you do think it might help us?"

Soon after Mr. Hayward returned to New York, we received the news that John Gruen would be ending his assignment in New Delhi and returning to New York. Glan Davies, who had retired from UNICEF and was now living in Britain, was to be the new regional director for India. John Gruen asked me to see him one evening after office hours. We had a drink in his office.

"Satish, you know by now that I am being transferred to New York. I wanted to tell you that I will seek early retirement before Christmas this year. I have long wanted to spend more time with my family and friends in Leiden. Please come and visit with us when you are next in Holland."

"I will certainly do so, John."

Before leaving his office, I asked him out of curiosity, "John, if you don't mind my asking, where did you like working the best in your long career?"

"Argentina and Guatemala. Argentina due to its cultural roots in Italy, and Guatemala for its hard-working people. In fact, Bhutan reminds me a little of Guatemala." John's candid response confirmed my instinct that a good man had been wasted working in the wrong cultural milieu.

There was good news on the family front. My father and mother had come to visit us. So did my father-in-law and mother-in-law. There were always a few relatives staying with us—some for medical treatments at the famous All India Institute of Medical Sciences (AIIMS), and others on religious pilgrimages to Hindu sacred sites across India. Our full house occasionally irritated me, but I also appreciated being able to keep up with family and friends after being far away for such a long time. Another positive aspect was that Sheila, being much more social than I, enjoyed hosting with warm hospitality. It also kept her busy during my frequent work trips all around South Asia.

The biggest source of joy was that Sheila was expecting our second child. By coincidence, Sheila's gynecologist was the same doctor who was looking after Indira Gandhi's daughter-in-law. We found this out when we went to her clinic for Sheila's checkups. There was a new red phone at the corner of Dr. Urmil Sharma's desk. It began to blink while we were there. Our doctor told us that it was a direct line to the prime minister's residence. Dr. Sharma was kind enough to give the number for the shiny red phone to Sheila, too.

Our son Samir was born on April 5, 1978. Thanks to the care of our family doctor Dr. Kul Bhusan Kapur, and Dr. Sharma, Sheila and Samir received world-class care and attention. Sheila's and my parents were delighted to welcome the new baby. I felt boundless joy.

I was able to work with three regional directors and two

executive directors during my assignments in India. It was a matter of good fortune that the state of emergency was withdrawn after Indira Gandhi was heavily defeated in the general election. The new democratic government released all political prisoners. Censorship of the news media was abolished. There was an air of dynamism and happiness at the restoration of democratic values.

We in the UNICEF India office were also relieved and happy to have Glan Davies at the helm. We prepared a five-year program of cooperation with the government, which was approved by the UNICEF board. Several elements of my message to Mr. Hayward were included in UNICEF's new program.

CHAPTER 26

My Deepest Sorrow

Nineteen eighty was an eventful year for me and for my family. My father passed away at the age of ninety-eight, in Bharatpur. Our family had moved from our ancestral home in Govindpur to a new place in Bharatpur, the major town in Chitwan. He had been living there for over 25 years. Sheila, whom he loved like a daughter, was with him at his deathbed. Upon learning of his illness, I was on my way to India from New York, and thanks to Sheila's presence of mind, she had even bought a ticket for me on a connecting flight to Kathmandu. I reached Kathmandu in time, but I could not get a car to drive the four hours' journey to Bharatpur in time. To my great sorrow, I was unable to be with him during his last moments. Sheila and other members of my family were waiting for me. After I arrived, we started the ritual of taking the dead body of my father to the bank of the river Narayani, close to our farmhouse. As per Nepali cultural practice, I spent the next thirteen days performing Hindu rites for the liberation of my father's soul.

During those thirteen days of sorrow and mourning, I reflected upon various facets of my father's personality, and recalled snippets of memories. I remembered that in 1979, I had met my father in what turned out to be our last meeting. In the course of our talk, he had strongly told me that he had anticipated his passing away rather soon.

"Babu, after I go away, please make sure that our daughter-in-law Sheila and you will look after your mom."

I tried to laugh away his suggestion that he would depart soon by saying, "Baba, I hope and strongly believe that you will be with us until you become a centenarian. Even our scriptures say "*Satam jivet.*" Being a spiritual person, you will certainly follow the scriptures' advice."

He replied, "Don't take my advice lightly. You may not be aware that our kith and kin are somewhat jealous of your prosperity. So they will make all kinds of demands and requests of your mother while you will be working abroad. So please take my advice seriously."

I then promised him that he should not be worried, and that my wife and I would devote more time and attention to the well-being of our mother.

The final talk between Baba and me turned out to be a prophetic direction in my later life. It guided my decision, to some extent, to move from China to Nepal in the mid 1980s.

Nineteen-eighty was also when James Grant was appointed as the third executive director of UNICEF. This was a major event in the life of the organization. I was very happy, as I had fond memories of our meetings and our discussions in New Delhi. I was aware of his ideological orientation and world outlook. Having worked with three regional directors and having attended several international meetings in New York and Geneva, I was also aware that the old guard and dead wood littered around UNICEF would give him a tough time.

As the new director, he visited some of the major country offices spread over different continents. He came to India, stayed at the Asoka Hotel, and held day-long meetings with the Delhi-based UNICEF staff. He invited ten senior officials, including Glan Davies and me, for a working lunch in his suite. I remember the occasion because Mr. Grant mentioned to Glan that he remembered me from his earlier visit.

"The then-regional director," he said smiling, "threw me out of his office, yet was graceful enough to arrange for coffee and snacks for me." All my colleagues, including Glan, looked at me intently. Ever since, I was branded "the blue-eyed boy of Jim Grant" despite my definitely dark-brown eyes, This meeting turned out to be almost like a seminar. Mr. Grant kept provoking us with difficult questions, and many of my colleagues who had grown up in the UNICEF work culture were either silent or subservient. I, on the other hand, with the help of a couple of drinks, was in rare intellectual form.

"Even if the entire budget of UNICEF were to be allocated to India, we still would only be making a marginal difference," I stated rather bluntly. "Instead, we should devise and implement an 'acupuncture approach' to programming. We need to reduce the bottlenecks and lessen the pain in selected points."

"How would you do it?" he asked me.

I spoke uninterruptedly for about 20 minutes. The whole time, Jim was focused and attentive. When I finished, Mr. Grant said, "Shall we finish our lunch?"

My colleagues were stunned at my audacity. When we came back to our office, one of my colleagues, a Swede named Karl Schoenmyer, told me, "Satish, we will either be dismissed after today's talk, or promoted very soon."

At the end of March 1981, I began to receive hints from UNICEF headquarters that Mr. Grant might appoint me UNICEF's representative to China. I was still in a sad frame of mind after Baba's death. I was closer to him than to my mother, and my inability to see him in his final moments hurt me deeply. I was still mourning his loss.

The prospect of working in China, with its ancient civilization and culture, and its huge population and innovative policy approaches, was exciting. Nepal has had relations with China and Tibet for centuries. Buddhism and Buddhist architecture from Nepal were introduced to China in these historical times. The famous architect Araniko was invited by Emperor Kublai Khan to build many Buddhist stupas in Beijing and the surrounding area. Similarly, a Nepali princess named Bhrikuti was married to the Tibetan emperor Songtsen Gampo. Given its strained cultural and political relationships with China's neighboring provinces, Tibet had always impressed me.

Late one evening, I received a call from Jim Grant informing me that he had selected me from among twenty candidates to serve as UNICEF's representative to China. He said a letter should be reaching me within the few days via UN Pouch, our internal mail system. I thanked him profusely and asked his advice about books I should read before reaching Beijing. He gave me the titles of half a dozen books and advised me to read a recently published multi-volume report from the World Bank.

The flow of congratulatory messages started, and I also sensed an element of envy among many of my colleagues in UNICEF. Sheila and I began the tasks of moving once again, this time from a country that was culturally and physically close to our homeland, to Beijing, a country that seemed exotic and new. Before leaving, we celebrated our son Samir's third birthday with our friends and their kids in Delhi, at a guest house because we had already packed up our residence.

CHAPTER 27

CHINA

"With leveled brow, I gaze at a thousand
accusing fingers. With bowed head I
serve the people like an ox."
—*Chinese author and poet, Lu Xun*

I WAS excited to represent UNICEF in the People's Republic.
Mao's China was beginning to open to the wider world. The
horrors of the Cultural Revolution were over. The capriciousness
of the Red Guards was replaced by rehabilitation. I was lucky
to have visited China in early 1979 as a member of a research
group funded by the World Health Organization, UN Food and
Agricultural Organization, and the United Nations Children's
Fund (UNICEF). The contrast between the hopeless attitude in
China immediately following the Cultural Revolution, and the
energy and can-do optimism of the early 1980s, was remarkable.

At the end of April 1981, we arrived in Beijing. At the airport, we were received by representatives of the Ministry of

International Relations and Trade, our contact organization in the government of China. In the lobby of the Beijing Hotel, we were received by two UNICEF colleagues bearing some fruit and a bouquet of flowers. This pattern of protocol, I found out later, was very common. The Chinese government's representatives would play the lead, and UNICEF would take a secondary role.

After we settled into our suite that evening, we came down to the dining room to eat dinner as a family. We were told that dinner was served between 5:00 and 7:00 pm, and after that, the restaurant was closed. We had come from the New Delhi tradition of late evening dinners at hotels, and were surprised to find that dinner services at a hotel for international visitors could be closed so early.

We were also struck by the fact that in a dining hall that could easily seat 120 people, there were only three tables with knives and forks—the rest were set with chopsticks. We were directed to one of the three "Western" dining tables, and the hostess told us that we should always seat ourselves at tables with forks and knives in the future. The meal was meager, with little choice. We ate whatever was served to us.

The next morning, during breakfast, the situation became even more bizarre. Sheila noticed a lady in the dining hall dressed in a colorful Indian sari with a large, vermillion tika on her forehead. In her resplendent dress, the lady looked regal. Sheila moved to greet her as a spontaneous gesture, spoke with her for a few minutes, and came back to inform me that she had just met a well-known classical dancer, invited by China's Ministry of Culture to perform in Beijing. Sheila told me that contrary to what we had heard in India, there seemed to be some cultural exchange and travel between India and China.

We ordered our breakfast. Our children were happily running between different tables. After half an hour or so, we heard a commotion coming from the Indian dancer's table. There was a sharp exchange of words between the waitress and the guest.

"This is not vegetarian soup!" the dancer shouted. "I don't eat meat or fish—only vegetables. I need a pure vegetarian breakfast."

"This is the soup we serve. If you want vegetarian, wait for a few minutes."

The waitress went to the kitchen and came back with a bowl, then she fished out all meat pieces from the soup. "There," she said, smiling. "Madam, you have your vegetarian soup now." The dancer was flabbergasted.

"All right, then, please give me some fruit."

"We don't serve fruit in the restaurant. There is a basket of fruit and a thermos of hot tea in your room."

The Indian lady left the dining room in anger. This exchange told us something about the limited nature of tourism and customer service in China in the early 1980s.

The UNICEF office was located in an area called Sanlitun, a neighborhood that had a number of embassies, including the embassy of Nepal. During the meet and greet with the staff and officials in the office, I asked them how long it would be before we could find private housing.

My two international colleagues remained silent, and the office's interpreter responded, "Sir, the housing situation is difficult in Beijing. Moreover, apartments are selected and given out by the Ministry of Housing with the approval of the Department of International Relations and Trade. We have already applied for an apartment for you, but it may take some time."

I remembered being exasperated by unwanted agents and brokers trying to rent apartments in New Delhi, and here I began to feel the same exasperation, but for the opposite reason, of having no control over finding housing for my family. We stayed at the Beijing Hotel for two months, at the end of which we were offered a one-bedroom apartment.

Weeks of official courtesy visits began, and so began what felt like an unending series of formal dinners at night. I noticed with amusement that in the Chinese administrative tradition, the hosts made a speech welcoming me, and in return, I also had to respond with a speech. I didn't mind speech-making, but I was struck by the Chinese system of serving sweet soup at the end of the banquet.

These official dinners were fun and a curiosity for Sheila and me. There were name cards written in Chinese in front of each guest's seat. My name therefore appeared in Chinese as "Pu-La-Ba-Si." Inevitably, there were small glasses of Maotai, the potent Chinese rice liquor, on the tables. There was a fantastic variety of food served, and Sheila learned very quickly to caution the hosts that we did not eat dogs, insects, or snake-tail soup. And, of course, being Hindu, we did not eat beef. The list of what we did eat might have been shorter. However, in spite of our caution, we slipped up once or twice, and after returning home Sheila would sigh, "*Hey, bhagwan*," "Oh, Lord." Very quickly we started to love the taste of Peking duck, steamed whole fish, and pigeon's egg. We were struck by the fact that the dinners we were invited to, although warmly hospitable, were always in public restaurants and never at anyone's home.

In the Chinese language, my title was *Dai Biao*, which meant "the boss." As a Nepalese national with working experience in Western Europe, I was surprised and often irritated by the complex process of building an open society in China, which at the time still felt very closed. There was a tendency to retain total control over the movement of foreigners and overseas Chinese, who had started returning in huge numbers to the motherland. The overseas Chinese were directed to live in special hotels on the outskirts of Beijing.

Foreigners were divided into two categories in Chinese perception: Caucasians of the "red-nosed" variety, and people from friendly countries in Africa, who were lavished with praise but viewed as being beneath Chinese dignity. It appeared to me that China was trying to integrate itself with the outer world, yet it remained afraid of being exploited and spied upon by foreigners.

China's history of a hundred years of humiliation before the Revolution affected every aspect of the Chinese psyche. The situation was further complicated by the fact that the more the Chinese saw advancement and progress in other countries, the more aware they became of how much they had to catch up.

Chinese leadership always remember fondly the foreigners who have helped China gain international recognition. They are called "friends of China." Dr Henry Kissinger is the most trusted friend in the eyes of Chinese leadership, as he was the prime motivator to facilitate the U.S. opening to China. I had read his memoir, *White House Years*, which had given me a fairly detailed knowledge of Dr. Kissinger's contribution to China's opening to the wider world. The Chinese leaders had a reverential friendship with Dr. Kissinger. As a token of their friendship to him, they used to invite him and his wife every couple of years. They would host a reception and sometimes, an official dinner, in honor of the power couple. The receptions were hosted in one of the remarkable rooms of the Great Hall of the People.

I was fortunate to be invited to one of the receptions in 1982 held in honor of their visit to China. My wife Sheila and I were excited, and felt honored to attend such a glorious gathering. The function started at six pm. There were a large number of limousines and cars. There was thorough vetting of the guests, and a close look at the invitation card that we had to carry.

Sheila and I walked into the Great Hall. I have a distinct memory of three things that struck me. There were over one thousand people invited, including civilian and military leadership of China, diplomatic representatives, ambassadors, first secretaries, etc., and journalists from both the U.S. and China. I had never seen such a mixed gathering of Chinese leaders, diplomatic representatives, and other dignitaries.

The Kissinger couple made it a point to circulate in the crowd, with the determination to shake hands with as many people as possible. Sheila and I were lucky to be amongst the first group of people to shake hands with the couple. Dr. Kissinger talked for a few minutes about Nepal and UNICEF's work in China. Once they moved on, I quickly dashed off to encourage the

Nepali Ambassador General Guna Shumsher Rana to meet Dr. Kissinger. I was surprised at my ambassador's reaction when he said, "I have nothing to discuss with him." I was perplexed and let it go.

In our UNICEF office, I tried to establish a tradition of bringing national staff into informal meetings and discussions. The Chinese nationals in my office were reluctant to participate in the beginning, and later on, when they did come, they would take extensive notes on what was said by the international staff in the room.

Once, I asked my interpreter, Mr. Wu, who had begun to warm up and feel a little friendlier to our family, "Why do you and your colleagues take so many notes?"

He was silent for a few minutes. After some reflection, he said, "Sir, we meet every Saturday afternoon, and all of us who work with foreigners have to report to our seniors about what is discussed and what is done in the office."

Mildly surprised, I asked him, "Mr. Wu, is that only for UNICEF, or for all the other agencies, too?"

He answered, "It is for every office—anywhere there are foreigners. We report on the work and activities every Saturday, and we have been told by our seniors that we should be friendly yet vigilant. We should try to help our international friends but maintain our distance, too. These issues are also brought up at the Saturday meetings."

Jokingly, I asked him, "So how many times have you criticized me at these meetings?"

He laughed, and said "It is not so personal, sir; it is mostly about foreign attitudes to China and policies being proposed."

There were many instances in my early years in China that verified and confirmed what Mr. Wu had told me. At the time, many office supplies were unavailable in Beijing, so a member of our staff would fly to Hong Kong and come back with essential supplies. Once, I came back from Hong Kong with varieties of chocolate and some colorful balloons for the children of our staff.

When my secretary and I started to give these small gifts to our colleagues, none of them accepted. They smiled politely but were adamant in refusing the gifts. I felt deflated by this and asked my friendly driver, Mr. Yan, "Why doesn't anyone take the chocolates and the small tokens for their children?"

Yan was a Buddhist and a kind-hearted man. The next day, he told me, "The problem of the gifts will be solved if you put everything on the table, display it, and tell us to take whatever we want."

I displayed all the chocolates and balloons on the conference table of our office and asked my secretary, Nicole, to inform everyone. Within two hours, the table was empty. It seemed to me that accepting gifts on an individual basis was a grave error, but something communal and public was acceptable. I thought to myself, "Even the old master Confucius would be at a loss in modern-day China."

Once, I brought a few things for the son of our *Ayi*, the woman assigned by the government to help us at home. She loved our children, and they reciprocated her love. I brought a few simple gifts for her son, which Sheila attempted to give her. Ayi adamantly refused. Sheila was confused and hurt. "Why won't you accept our gifts?" she kept asking.

There were tears in Ayi's eyes when she answered, "Madam, you are kind, but you don't know that the elevator woman is from the internal security service. If she saw me taking a package from your apartment, she would be duty bound to inform her boss. I would lose my job."

She also suggested a way out. "Madam, if one of you were to leave the building a little before me, with the package, and wait for me outside the compound gate, I would be happy to receive your gift, and my son would be happy, too." Accordingly, Sheila left with the package one afternoon, waited for Ayi, and surreptitiously handed over the gift for her young son.

Mr. Wu, my interpreter, and Mr. Yan, our office driver, became my best friends and my guides to social and cultural behavior in

Beijing. One day, Mr. Yan was driving me to the office. On the way, there was a big walled compound that Mr. Yan had told me was the second biggest court in Beijing. When we were driving past, we heard sporadic bursts that sounded like fireworks coming from the direction of the courthouse.

"Is today a festival?"

"No."

"What is this noise, then?" I asked him.

"Shoot," Mr. Yan replied.

Having just come from India, where Bollywood reigns supreme, I asked him, "Oh, so there is some filming going on? It happens mostly in Bombay and New Delhi in India."

"No, not film. Shoot."

Totally puzzled, I asked him, "What shoot?"

Yan took one of his hands off the steering wheel and pointed two fingers to his temple. "Like this."

There was a notice in our newspaper, he said, that the court would not be working today and that people should not come to the courthouse. Instead, today there would be action against criminals.

"How many?" I asked.

"Hundred and fifty," he said. "Many of them sentenced to die some years ago but the real shooting happening today."

I was stunned. I wondered, "What was UNICEF doing here? What was I doing here?"

My two children, Sarina and Samir, were enrolled in the International School of Beijing. As the school did not have its own building, it operated out of a property owned by the American embassy, only a few minutes away from our apartment. The children rode their bikes to school. My wife, Sheila, joined Beijing University for a year-long Chinese-language course. Given her excellent handwriting, she became a neat calligrapher. Sheila had earlier discovered an aptitude for languages, when, in the Netherlands, she had become more proficient in Dutch than I, though I had lived there much longer. Sheila's sociable personality, her curiosity, and her knack for learning languages served us all well as we adjusted to our life in Beijing.

She became very popular in her class, so we wanted to invite her teachers and classmates to our home. Her classmates were delighted to accept her invitation. The faculty members, however, said they would have to get permission from the Ministry of Culture, as the university was affiliated to this ministry. We were quite confident that permission would be granted for dinner at one of the students' apartments. However, it took approximately three months before they received clearance to attend the dinner.

Sheila's language proficiency sometimes created problems for us. Whenever we would go to social functions organized by the Chinese government, Mr. Wu and some of the other Chinese guests would be informed that Mrs. Prabasi spoke Chinese very well and that they should compliment her.

Out of curiosity, one day I asked Mr. Yan why my wife was praised for speaking the Chinese language whenever there were Chinese guests with us. Mr. Yan smiled.

"Dai Biao, this is a polite way of informing the gathering that they should not speak of serious matters in her presence. They know that you don't understand Chinese, so they can speak freely and speak their minds, but because of Madam, they have to be cautious."

Distilling my experiences in different countries, and analyzing the social situation I observed in China, I devised a three-pronged strategy for UNICEF's work. The first was accepting and emphasizing the fact that China was too vast, with huge resources of its own, for UNICEF to help the government in any impactful financial way. UNICEF could only be effective in reducing points of pain and filling in the gaps that had occurred primarily due to the Cultural Revolution. I wanted to identify selected areas of cooperation, where UNICEF would develop what I called an "acupunctural approach to programming," pinpointing the areas where we wanted to have an impact. This would require extensive and honest discussions with friends in the government to specify our course of action.

The second approach was that, in China, with its 5,000 years of history and deep memories of past glory and recent humiliation, UNICEF would not pontificate about what needed to be done. Instead, we would jointly select points in the body politic of China to treat current deficiencies. For instance, China had decided on four focuses for modernization: agriculture, industry, science and technology, and defense. Given UNICEF's mandate, we could not work in defense or science and technology, but we could partner with the government to promote education for women and children and provide opportunities to study abroad; the Chinese government could choose how to capitalize on these initiatives. I told my counterparts in the Chinese government that UNICEF in general—and I myself—were deeply aware of the damage done to higher education and teachers' training programs during the excesses of the Cultural Revolution. One could develop a program for study abroad by coordinating with teachers and scholars who were persecuted by the Red Guards.

I was also aware that thousands of libraries across China were destroyed during that period. I suggested a program focused on rehabilitating libraries and rejuvenating rural primary-health institutions in selected counties.

The third prong would be paying extra attention to the advancement of minority groups. I appreciated that minority groups had received ideological support from Chairman Mao. There were then fifty-five officially recognized minority groups in China, with a combined population of 84 million. For these demographic groups, the government of China had not imposed the one-child policy, and consequently, the minority population had grown much faster than the national average. I wanted UNICEF's program to support health, education, and women's welfare among the minority groups. 84 million did not sound like a large part of China's population, but for UNICEF's program and budget, it was a very significant number.

Through wide-ranging discussions, I received the government's blessing to focus UNICEF's program on twenty-seven of the most underdeveloped counties that had large minority populations. To my great satisfaction, these included some of the most marginalized populations, including the cave-dwellers of Yunan Province, the Tibetan highlanders in the windswept province of Qinghai, and the tent-dwelling people of the steppes of Inner Mongolia.

It was my great fortune that James Grant supported my approach to our projects in China, and UNICEF's focus on helping the most deprived people. During my stay in China, I received intellectual and moral support from three strong personalities: James Grant; Soong Ching-ling, the wife of Sun Yat-sen; and a Canadian–Chinese man named Paul Lin.

Jim was an extraordinary person, with great vision for the advancement of women and children. He was born in China in 1922, where his father had worked for many years as a missionary doctor. Jim used to tell me, "Satish, I am a 'MisKid'—a missionary kid. I therefore have a great passion for my work." When James Grant joined UNICEF as the organization's third executive director in 1980, he brought an American version of the revitalization of UNICEF as an organization. He shook up the lethargic work style of UNICEF by bringing in fresh blood and new ideas. He did not talk about improvement in terms of percentages; he constantly talked about shifting gears and moving from the first gear of UNICEF's existence to the third or even fourth. And this was the time of Ronald Reagan and Margaret Thatcher, neither of whom could be called, by any stretch of the imagination, friends of the poor.

As a result, international funding and even policy support for women and children in the Third World was placed on the backburner, and the Falklands War and Star Wars were the priorities of the British and American governments. In this period of international stagnation and dwindling government resources, Jim Grant started speaking at various international forums and at UNICEF about the fact that 15 million children under the age of five died each year, though there was no reason for them to die. His friend and professional colleague, Peter Adamson, wrote many years later, "Rather than motivating his audience, with his talk of shifting gears, he succeeded mainly in mystifying and alarming them." Some colleagues even began to fear for the sanity of their new boss, Adamson recounts.

Jim's passion for the larger view of development and his emphasis on low-cost approaches to child health led to a direct confrontation with the World Health Organization (WHO), who thought of themselves as the father and godfather of anything health-related. The WHO was headed by a Danish doctor named Halfdan Mahler. He made no secret of his contempt for Jim Grant's approach to child survival and ridiculed Jim's emphasis on a few drops to prevent diphtheria and a salt-and-sugar solution to end diarrhea. In 1983, Halfhan Mahler gave a speech to distinguished delegates of the WHO, which became known as the "parachute-red herring speech."

"I'm all for impatience if it leads to speedier action. But I am against it if it imposes fragmented action from above. I am refer-ring to such initiatives as the parachuting of foreign agents into developing countries to immunize them from above, [or] the con-centration on only one aspect of diarrheal disease control without thought for others. Initiatives such as these are red herrings."

Undeterred, Jim started a global campaign called the Child Survival Revolution. But he also faced internal, organizational opposition. Some ancient regional directors began to joke that Jim wanted to promote "tits for tots" and that his blue-eyed boy in China was all for it. Despite internal opposition and interagency rivalry, Jim, to my great appreciation, promoted a five-cent solution to child mortality in the Third World. Adamson wrote later, "Even Thatcher and Reagan could not ignore the argument that no child should die for lack of a five-cent vaccine." Jim's background, having worked with USAID and the Overseas Development Council, helped him raise funds in many countries, and the Child Survival Revolution had a firm footing at UNICEF.

It has been said that high ambition has high costs. Jim's passion and his complete belief in his strategy for promoting child survival took a toll on him. His wife died of a heart attack during one of his visits to India. After that, Jim became lonely and forlorn.

The degree of animosity toward me and my work in China increased in proportion to Jim's success with his Child Survival Strategy. I was, however, protected to some extent by the support and warm appreciation I received from the China Soong Ching-ling Foundation in Shanghai. Paul Lin was the man who introduced me to the foundation. Professor Lin, a Canadian citizen and a truly progressive Chinese man at heart, had been, I found out, a close family friend of Zhou Enlai, the first Premier of the People's Republic of China, and his wife. Thanks to his contacts, I was able to interface with the China Soong Ching-ling Foundation. We discovered a common interest in promoting the welfare and development of children in minority-populated areas. Through UNICEF, I was able to support Paul's documentary filmmaking in Yunan Province. I was honored to discover that I was acknowledged in Paul and Eileen Lin's book, *In the Eye of the China Storm*.

During my three years in China, Jim came to Beijing six times. Each of his visits helped me promote UNICEF's programs. Instead of being just my boss, he became a close friend of our family who looked forward to "fusion Asian" meals prepared by Sheila, who would marvel at his ability to eat a copious amount of green chilies. One time when I went to his hotel room to pick him up, I was astonished to see him washing his underclothes in the hotel bathroom.

"Jim, what are you doing? There are plenty of laundry services in Beijing," I blurted out in shock.

"Oh, Satish, you don't realize that some missionary habits never die."

During my almost ten years of work living and working in India and China I observed many similarities and some distinct differences.

I observed some similarities between India and China. Most notable was the moral and ethical prominence given to the role of women and girls in both societies. China would emphasize through propaganda Mao's dictum that "Women hold up half the sky," and in India, the goddess called Durga is worshipped each year during the festival of Dussehra. Female deities abound in India, and in China, so do the statues of Guan Yin, the goddess of mercy and compassion. Yet in practice, in both countries, women and girls continue to be mistreated. Infanticide of girls was common in both countries; the preference for a male child is pronounced in both cultures.

There were contrasts in their policies, though. Both countries had huge rural populations. The common problem of managing people's migration from rural areas to small towns and urban centers was a daunting task. But their approaches were completely different. The Chinese government followed a strict policy of "in-place" development, which meant that the rural population was not allowed to move to urban centers without the express consent of commune officials. This led to some very harsh, even inhuman, outcomes. The most glaring example was that spouses working in different locations were not allowed to leave their places of work more than twice a year. In my own office, Mr. Wu could visit his wife in Shanghai only once every six months.

In India, the boy's family demands huge amounts of dowry for marrying the girl of a given family. These days, they even demand a color television or a car, depending upon the economic status of the girl's family. Many poor families in India have been economically ruined by these demands for dowry.

Strict family planning was applied in both countries. In the case of India, there was a popular slogan, "We two, our two," promoting two-child families. China went further and imposed the one-child policy. In both countries, statistics had to be taken with a grain of salt. Data was suspect—government data even more so.

My third year in China was momentous and shattering. A combination of personal and institutional factors precipitated my departure from China and UNICEF.

There was a house-warming party in 1981 after the Chinese government allocated a new building for UNICEF, with a lovely garden surrounding it. The party turned out to be memorable, with hundreds of guests, whom I called friends of UNICEF. It was graced by the Chinese foreign minister Hwang Hua, and our Executive Director Jim Grant. I was fortunate to have known the foreign minister thanks to Professor Lin, who met him in Canada. There were more than a hundred guests. Jim's presence at the inauguration added luster to the party. The event was high-lighted in the national press in Beijing and at UNICEF.

I was invited to our head office in New York to attend a UNICEF board meeting that approved a nine-million-dollar program of cooperation with the government of China. It included support for the education and heath sectors, especially in twenty districts populated by minority ethnic groups. There was also a high degree of emphasis on educational exchange—visits by Chinese officials to selected western universities and institutions. I was especially pleased to promote this cultural exchange.

But in the meantime, I was getting upset and emotionally disturbed by weekly telephone calls from Kathmandu. My mother and other relatives urgently implored me to return to Nepal. My mother was getting very old, and this had begun to weigh on my mind. I began pondering my father's last request—that I should look after my mother after he passed away.

I had continued supporting my relatives financially, but now my mother wanted me to come home. Moreover, I began to suffer from increasing mental fatigue. These factors precipitated my move away from the organization I cherished so deeply, and from some of my friends, like Jim, who had become like family to me. I remembered my urge, two decades before, to leave Kathmandu and explore the world.

In those days UNICEF's headquarters was located in the Alcoa Building by the East River in New York. I have many sweet memories of that neighborhood. My wife and young children had occasionally rented an apartment in Beekman Plaza. I used to take my young son Samir in a stroller in the surrounding little parks.

A major change in my life came when I was in the Alcoa Building, on one of the missions from China to New York. I decided to quit my job in order to go back to Nepal, via the Netherlands.

CHAPTER 28

REDISCOVERING NEPAL

Iᴛ was pleasant to come back to the Kathmandu Valley after spending almost two decades abroad. Sarina was ten years old, Samir was five, and having grown up outside Nepal, they had children's curiosity and an innocent wonder at seeing their ancestral land. We had found a Nepali tutor who would teach Sarina and Samir how to read and write in Nepali. We spoke Nepali at home, and they were conversationally fluent but had never learned to read or write the script.

Sarina and Samir were adjusting to many changes. My young son asked me, "Daddy, why are all these people wearing an elephant necklace?" He was referring to the lockets depicting Lord Ganesh that he saw many people wearing.

One day, I remember an outburst by both of them about our daily lunch and dinner of *dal-bhat*, rice and lentils: "*Dal-bhat, dal-bhat*, why always *dal-bhat*?" Having been used to a wide variety of foods from our travels and from our adopted custom of "fusion-food," our kids couldn't imagine the constant meals of rice and lentils in the life of the average Nepali family. It was a big readjustment for Sheila, too, who had the still-quite-traditional social expectations of a middle-class Nepali wife thrust upon her.

The changes in the center of Kathmandu were even more striking. The quiet, wide Dharmapath, where I used to walk during my student days, now led to an infamous street catering to tourists called "Freak Street." The junction of Dharmapath and Freak Street truly freaked me out. Foreign tourists and young Nepalis were often imbibing intoxicants of all varieties as part of their spiritual quests.

We lived in the picturesque little neighborhood of Mahankal, a ten-minute walk from the famous Boudhanath temple complex on the northeastern outskirts of Kathmandu. There are different origin stories for the construction of Boudhanath. Most credible to me is that the Tibetan king, Songtsen Gampo, built the first stupa sometime around the year 600, after he converted to Buddhism, as an act of devotion. Boudhanath had grown into a massive center of Tibetan refugees and western tourists, along with a smaller number of foreigners seriously studying Tibetan Buddhism.

The massive, rounded, luminous stupa with all-seeing eyes is the largest in Nepal, and in the winter, thousands of Tibetan pilgrims come from India and the neighboring Tibetan districts of Nepal to pay respects and offer prayers. In 1979, it was declared a UNESCO World Heritage Site. We were enchanted by the rhythm and lyrics of the Buddhist mantra, "*Om mani padme hum*," "The jewel is in the lotus." We admired the Buddhist prayer wheels spinning around the massive structure. Colorful prayer flags fluttered in the breeze. The hustle and bustle of shops and vendors encircled the stupa.

Our house in Boudhanath was also close to Kapan Monastery. It was established in the 1960s by Tibetan lamas and spiritual gurus with the twin objectives of serving as a retreat to Tibetan "seekers" and the foreign followers of Lama Zopa Rinpoche and Lama Yeshe. There were hundreds of short-term Buddhist visitors from Colorado and California and from Rome and Venice. Many of them had rented rooms on a short-term basis in our house in Boudhanath. This gave Sheila and me an opportunity to renew contacts with our European and American friends and to learn more about Tibetan Buddhism. We recall with pleasure many disciples and scholars of Buddhism who came from the Naropa Institute in Boulder, Colorado. Thanks to these contacts, we were privileged to host the Lama Zopa Rinpoche for dinner at our home.

Sheila and I decided that we should take our children to some of the cultural landmarks in the city and to cultural heritage sites around the country. One sunny morning, we took our children to Swayambhunath. It is known among visiting tourists and children alike as "the Monkey Temple." There is a series of Buddhist monasteries, small and formidable, in the complex. In Nepali, its name means "self-sprung," and in Tibetan, it is known as Singgu, which means "sublime tree." Many of the temples and shrines are believed to have been built during the Lichchhavi period of the Kathmandu Valley, which existed from approximately the years 400 to 750. If Boudhanath is known as the largest Buddhist stupa, Swayambhunath is best known for housing the biggest *vajra*—the thunderbolt scepter of both Hindu and Buddhist mythology. Swayambhunath's architecture belongs to the Bajrayana tradition of the Newar Buddhist community of Kathmandu Valley. The site is also revered by Hindu pilgrims.

During these visits, we wanted to impress upon our children that Nepal's cultural traditions and its history have been inclusive, and religious groups have been both tolerant of and deeply influenced by each other.

The small mountain kingdoms of Nepal were gradually annexed by a larger kingdom governed by the Shah dynasty, the Kingdom of Gorkha. We wanted our children to visit the ancient and decaying palace of Gorkha. During a school holiday, we drove up to the town center. We started our climb up a series of stone steps to the palace. After climbing a couple of hundred steps, our son, Samir, absolutely refused to climb any farther. After much cajoling from all of us, he reluctantly agreed to keep walking.

We reached the entrance of the palace and requested of the chief priest that we be allowed to see the sacred room. The place was dark, so we also asked for a lantern or some other kind of light. Instead, he merely asked us if we had brought a flashlight. We were utterly disappointed at the state of disrepair and neglect of one of Nepal's key historic sites. The Palace of Prithvi Narayan Shah, who had unified Nepal into one country, could not be viewed without a flashlight.

Our return to our car was equally startling. We were all fatigued, and at one point we saw a lady chaffing corn on her round woven tray, called a *nanglo*. The children wanted a snack and were thirsty from all the walking.

I asked the woman politely, "Didi, can we buy some corn and get a jug of water? The children are hungry and thirsty."

She smiled at me and said, "Dai, you don't need to buy corn; I'll gladly give it to you. But water you should not take from me."

"Why?" I asked, perplexed.

"I belong to the *kami* caste," she said, referring to the black-smith caste, considered impure and untouchable. "If people see me offering you water, I will be punished, and you will be scolded."

Sheila and I were stunned into silent despair. Having traveled the world as a promoter of equality, I found it a stark reminder of the situation at the heart of my own country.

"My children are thirsty. Please give us a jug of water."

She looked around, and not seeing anyone, almost surreptitiously put a jug of water in front of us. She was visibly anxious for us to leave. Sheila thanked her profusely, and then we continued our descent to the town where our car was parked. When we reached the car, I couldn't wait to get out of there.

When we reached Kathmandu, I made it a point to meet with Mr. John Ritter, who was the Director of the international school in Kathmandu, the Lincoln School. I had met him in Beijing at the newly expanding American school where my daughter Sarina was enrolled. Mr. Ritter had agreed to enroll Sarina and Samir and receive payment in Nepalese currency, which was a huge relief to me.

"Mr. Ritter, I wanted to thank you for including the annual treks into the school program and syllabus."

"It is the highlight of our year, Mr. Prabasi, but why do you say this?"

"It means my children will learn more about Nepal than I did."

My three years in Beijing had convinced me of Mao's dictum that individuals and societies should walk on two legs. In the case of China, this meant agriculture and industry. I thought mine should be entrepreneurship and academic consultancies to keep me in the mainstream of development studies. Our first few weeks in Kathmandu were a flurry of family and friends, who welcomed us warmly with traditional Nepalese hospitality.

My priority had been to enroll our children at the Lincoln School, which was now done. My second priority was to reassure my mother that I was going to remain in Nepal for the foreseeable future, so she did not have to worry about being forsaken and lonely. I then began to explore the possibilities of business and consultancy.

CHAPTER 29

THE ROAD TO HELL IS PAVED WITH GOOD INTENTIONS

SOME of my friends from my earlier time in Nepal's government, notably Dirgha Raj Koirala, the Chief Secretary of the government, remembered my work in the Ministry of Agriculture. He invited me to join the board of directors of the Nepal Agricultural Bank; I accepted. Mr. Koirala, who was a strict vegetarian, told me to promote the dairy industry because Nepal had a big deficit in milk production, and this could help boost the incomes of many farmers in Nepal.

I had a small farm in the Chitwan district in southern Nepal, where my parents had lived for many years before Baba's death. There I registered a private company called Trise Dairy. The name stood for the names of two rivers in central Nepal, Trishuli and Seti. The Agricultural Development Bank took the initiative, with my encouragement, to seek a soft loan from the Asian Development Bank in order to lend money to small farmers with an emphasis on dairy development, in addition to the cultivation of cash crops. With a loan amounting to $10 million, we promoted the Small Farmers Development Project (SFDP).

During the first couple of years, the new dairy production on my farm in Chitwan thrived. Then unforeseen problems hit us. Though I had good theoretical knowledge of agricultural economics thanks to my studies in England, I failed miserably to appreciate that in the context of the Nepalese agricultural sector, theories did not coincide with reality. A few examples: in my dairy, I imported half a dozen of an improved breed of cows called Holstein Friesians. They were beautiful, black-and-white cows with extraordinary milk yields of twenty or more liters per animal per day. These animals needed to be fed high-energy feed, which was available from a factory nearby. The farmers from Chitwan and the surrounding area used to come and visit our dairy and would be amazed that an animal could yield so much milk. They asked me about the feed for the animals. They even asked me to help import some of these cows from India through the Agricultural Development Bank, which the bank was more than happy to do through the Small Farmers Development Project. Then, disaster struck. When the farmers found out that the cattle feed included processed animal bones, the traditionalist Hindu farmers were very angry. They blamed the bank and, especially, me.

"How can you feed holy creatures like cows this kind of food? How can a cow be fed with animal bones? This makes the animal and the milk impure!"

The farmers began to boycott the Agricultural Development Bank-assisted SFDP. In addition, they refused to feed their animals the high-energy feed; without the proper nutrition, the high-yield animals soon began to produce less milk.

I thought a solution for our dairy could be the processing of milk into dairy products like yogurt and traditional sweets loved in Nepal and India. So I established two outlets for the sale of these products. One was in the tourist area of eastern Chitwan called Tandi, where foreign and Indian tourists used to watch the wildlife. The other was in the main town called Narayanghat.

I hired some traditional confectioners from Bihar. When they came and started making yogurt and sweets, they found that the milk produced at our dairy was of good quality, but the milk we collected from neighboring farmers had been diluted with inordinate quantities of water, which affected the quality of the sweets. Rai-ji, the master sweet-maker, once related to me with great surprise and animation the story of a farmer who brought in his milk, and when it was being measured, a small fish jumped out of the container.

Consequently, Trise Dairy suffered over time from increasing levels of interest to repay the bank and dwindling revenues. This was the surest way to end up in hell, despite my good intentions.

While teaching in the Netherlands, I used to say jokingly that an unsuccessful businessman becomes a good consultant. He can then, as a consultant, explain the risks and opportunities in theory. I therefore decided to become a consultant rather than a businessman and established a consultancy firm called CERES: The Center for Regional and Ecological Studies. Given my background and résumé, many donor agencies working in Nepal, including USAID, Danish Aid (DANIDA), and the Dutch Voluntary Aid Group, SNV, signed contracts with CERES. We were quite successful as a consulting firm, but the nature of consultancy in Nepal was cyclical and not a steady stream of income.

I found a remarkable mix of approaches to development when working for small aid agencies in Nepal. I met many remarkable people, but two of them stand out in my memory.

Since I had spent so much time in the Netherlands, I made a courtesy call to the then-Country-Representative of SNV, Hans Reinveldt. A young man in his mid-thirties, Hans turned out to be a warm person interested in the development and growth of people who had been left behind. He had a lovely family, a wife and two children. He was a graduate of Rotterdam University and had taken a couple of courses with my mentor Jan Tinbergen. He told me that nongovernmental Dutch aid was geared toward fostering community participation in projects.

Rob Thurston was the chief of rural development at USAID. He had worked in Latin America and India prior to his assignment in Nepal. A tall man with a great sense of humor and engaging personality, Rob and I clicked. Soon, he offered me small-scale consultancies within his unit and invited me to be on the team of evaluators composed for the five western districts, the Rapti Integrated Development Project (RIDP) in western Nepal. Out of these five districts, two were heavily infested with Maoist guerrillas, and violent conflicts were on the rise.

Oftentimes I felt that the hidden assumption behind the RIDP was that USAID would be able to win over the hearts and minds of the population from the spreading influence of the guerrillas. Rob's experience in Colombia and Guatemala had given him experience and expertise in reaching out to uncommitted but vulnerable people. He and his wife liked Sheila and me, and we started socializing over dinner at each other's homes. Rob had traveled extensively to the most rural and remote hilled areas of Nepal, and in fact, he opened my eyes to the extent of poverty and degradation in some parts of our society.

This resulted in an anomalous situation in which I became quite popular with the donor community as a consultant, but I could not generate sufficient income to keep qualified staff at CERES. I learned about sericulture—the farming of silkworms and silk—from the Lutheran World Service; Angora rabbit farming from the Danes; beekeeping and honey from the Dutch; and eco-tourism from Canadians led by their Resident Consul. While I benefitted from this exposure, my personal financial situation continued to deteriorate, so much so that sometimes I felt like I was surrounded by insurmountable walls.

As my financial situation deteriorated, I had no option other than to begin selling off my assets and property to pay off loans and maintain a modest living. I was happy, though, that my children were in the international school. Sarina, through her own efforts, had applied to several colleges in the United States and had been accepted to Smith College with a significant scholarship.

I will never forget when I invited some of my prominent friends to dinner. Prime Minister Krishna Prasad Bhattarai came, and being a practical politician, he asked me how much I would have to pay to send Sarina to Smith College for four years. When I told him that she had a scholarship, so my contribution would not be more than $20,000 over four years, he nearly dropped his fork and exclaimed, "Why are you spending so much money on a girl's education? Don't you know she will marry and join another household? You are throwing away your money!"

I cursed inwardly, and thought to myself, "If this is the thinking of a prime minister of my country, what about the average, less educated people?" I also vowed to never invite that man to dinner at my home again.

As Sarina was packing and preparing for her departure to the United States during the summer of 1991, I gave her a miniature statue of Lord Buddha. I recall that I carried a similar statue with me when I was going to the United Kingdom for my own higher education. I was glad to notice that the statue I gave Sarina still adorns her bookshelf in her apartment in Manhattan.

Samir turned out to be an independent thinker. While Sarina was in Massachusetts, he visited his sister, and when he returned, he told me emphatically that he would not go to the U.S. for further studies. As I knew the Australian Ambassador, Brendan Doran, I thought our friendship might be helpful in facilitating a student visa for Samir. I was happy at last that, although our economic situation had declined, my children were gaining an education with a global outlook.

Tensions mounted within the family as our financial situation became direr by the day. Sending Samir to Australia was my last Herculean push. Given the cultural norms and expectations of a Nepali family, I, as the only son, could not leave my widowed mother. This felt like another insurmountable obstacle.

And then my mother died. It hurts me to say it, but her death at the age of 96 liberated me. It confirmed a prediction she often made to Sheila: "I know you and Sanobabu will leave Nepal within a few weeks of my death." It also reminded me of a passage by William Somerset Maugham.

You will hear people say that poverty is the best spur to the artist. They have never felt the iron of it in their flesh. They do not know how mean it makes you. It exposes you to endless humiliation, it cuts your wings, it eats into your soul like a cancer. It is not wealth one asks for, but just enough to preserve one's dignity, to work unhampered, to be generous, frank, and independent.

I thought how prescient he was. As was my habit, in times of depression and difficulty, I surrounded myself with books. In those days, I went back to William Somerset Maugham's seminal works, *Of Human Bondage* and *The Razor's Edge*. I sold my last remaining property, the home in Bharatpur, to a private buyer, a builder-contractor, at a throwaway price. It still wasn't enough. Sheila, worried about my declining health, physical and mental, convinced me to go to the U.S. Sarina, recently graduated, was living and working in Washington, D.C., with an international development nonprofit called Pact. Sheila would join me later, but took on the arduous and painful tasks of closing up our life in Nepal, and ending a particularly difficult chapter of our life together.

CHAPTER 30

A NOMADIC LIFE

For the next ten years, Sheila and I lived a nomadic life. During this period, we spent time in Washington, D.C., in Calcutta, and in Melbourne. Sheila and I were trying to recover from the trauma of leaving Nepal and losing so much. We were just beginning to settle into a new routine in Washington in 2001, when one day I received a phone call from the George Washington Hospital. The doctor asked me to come to the hospital because Sheila was there and wanted to consult with me. I was surprised and worried, and went to the hospital immediately. There, I found Sheila looking panicked and almost in tears.

"She says I have breast cancer. How can that be?" she blurted out as soon as she saw me. The young doctor talked with me privately, and told me that while the cancer had been detected in the early stages, it was best treated as soon as possible. She needed surgery, and then the doctors would decide the next course of action.

Sheila was devastated by her diagnosis. Cancer is a scary word, and suddenly it had come into our lives and into our daily vocabulary. I tried to focus on the positive. I told myself, and I told Sheila, that since the cancer had been diagnosed at such an early stage, there was no reason why she would not recover fully if we acted immediately. The silver lining in this emerging situation was that I had good-quality health insurance through the work that I had recently started on a short-term assignment with The Pearl S. Buck Foundation. This meant that Sheila would have the best treatment, which was a huge relief in an otherwise very precarious time.

The surgery went well, and I accompanied Sheila for her six weeks of follow-up radiation therapy. At the end of Sheila's treatment, the oncologist advised us that although all had gone as well as it could, Sheila would still need regular monitoring and follow-up for at least five years to ensure there would be no recurrence. After some discussion, we decided to move to Calcutta, India, where the cost of living was low but the quality of medical attention would be world class. Sheila's oncologist referred us to a specialist in Calcutta.

Another phase of our nomadic life began. With the help of a few friends in Calcutta, we found a lovely, affordable apartment in a new development called Salt Lake City. It was located on the eastern side of Calcutta, and planned by a well-known Yugoslav urban planner. In sharp contrast to the perceived image of the dirty city of Calcutta, Salt Lake City was clean, with small parks, residential blocks, and a public transportation system. Above all, our landlord, Mr. Ajit Kapas, had just retired from the position of Chief Secretary of the government of West Bengal. He was fond of Bengali and English literature. It was, again, our good luck that we found a kind and helpful landlord who eventually became a family friend.

On my early morning walks, I discovered a huge park near the official residence of the chief minister, Jyoti Basu. Mr. Basu was a scotch-loving Communist who loved a drink or two in the evening and who spent a month each summer in London. The park across the street from his residence was well maintained, and for some odd reason, it was called the Central Park. I loved walking in Central Park in the morning for its delightful scenes. In addition to the roses and tropical plants, I saw yoga groups, laughter ringing out from groups of elderly people practicing "laughing yoga," and small assemblies of Hindu devotees chanting hymns.

One drizzly morning, I sat down on a stone bench in the park, waiting to return home after the rain stopped. A lean, tall gentleman came and sat down beside me. After a couple of moments of silence, he said, "I could introduce you to a very spiritual guru, as you seem to be inclined towards spirituality."

I was taken aback. "I am more interested in physical wellbeing at the moment, but I wouldn't mind the guru if you think it would be worthwhile."

The gentleman introduced himself, "I'm Singh. If you'd like, I could show you another park tomorrow." Mr. Ganesh Prasad Singh turned out to be a retired director at Coal India Limited, one of the biggest companies in India.

"Sure. How about we meet at this spot tomorrow, and then you can take me to the other park?"

The next morning, Mr. Singh took me to a nearby park, about fifteen minutes' walk from the Central Park. There, I met a person of average height, completely dressed in sky-blue, with large, bright eyes. He was introduced to me simply as Guru-ji. He asked me some probing questions, and some simpler ones.

"I hold spiritual discussions in the evenings from 7:00 to 9:00 P.M. on different chapters of the holy book, the *Gita*. Do you know about the *Gita*?" he asked me kindly.

"I have read it, but I do not recite it regularly," I replied.

His following two questions startled me. "What is the purpose of life, do you think?"

"Depends on what you want to do."

His next question was even more enigmatic. "What do you think would have happened if you and I were not born?" I was not sure whether he was joking or serious and was unsure of how to answer.

I told him honestly, "I really don't know, except perhaps there would be less problems in Calcutta."

His final question was, "Why are you interested in spirituality?"

"Guru-ji, I am not a very spiritual man, but my life in the past few years has made me question some assumptions about life. So I want to study to understand philosophically, but not practice as a religious devotee."

I think he was pleased with my candor. He said, "Satish-ji, I would be glad if you joined our study group in the evenings, with two conditions. Punctuality—coming on time—and committing to continue with us for the first six chapters of the holy book."

"Why six chapters, Guru-ji?"

"The holy book is divided into eighteen chapters. To understand and appreciate the teachings and its messages, one has to follow at least one-third of it."

That sounded very logical to me, and this is how I began my association with Guru-ji, who over time became a spiritual guide to Sheila and me. He also led me to some holy places such as Rishikesh, a city I remembered as the place where the Beatles spent some time and learned the sitar, and where another guru famous in the western world, called Maharishi, had a cave with eighty-four rooms. It would not be wrong to say that I learned a lot and got to understand, partially, the rehabilitative value of Hindu philosophy.

Guru-ji helped Sheila, too. He gave her Ayurvedic remedies and taught her some yoga postures that would bring relief to her growing arthritis. I remember Guru-ji for some of his special qualities and habits. He adamantly refused to accept fees or payments. He would suggest, "Bring some fruit, and distribute it to the homeless."

Usually the park would get dark in the evening, so he wanted each one of us to bring a flashlight to take notes if we wanted to, and to arrive exactly on the dot at 7:00 pm. We could stay on later after 9:00 pm if we so wished, but we had to arrive exactly on time. Each evening, he used to carry six to eight large bottles of water from his own apartment and ask us to drink water before he started his discourse. Over time, I found out that according to Guru-ji, giving drinking water to others was the highest offering one could make. Occasionally, he would give us spiritual books such as the *Gita* and books on Vedanta, a Hindu school of philosophy.

In Hindu tradition, it is believed that on a day called Guru-Purnima, on the full moon, one should meet one's guru and get his blessings. Sheila and I try to follow this tradition even now, wherever we are, offering our greetings by phone when it is not possible in person.

Once, I went to visit Guru-ji in Rishikesh on Guru-Purnima. It was rainy season, so after a couple of delays on the train track, we reached the station in Hardwar, another holy town on the way to Rishikesh. I stayed overnight there and called Guru-ji to inform him that I was on my way. I requested him to arrange a room for me at the ashram, one with hot water and a Western-style toilet. It turned out that there were only three rooms out of over 120 that had a Western-style toilet, and luckily for me, Guru-ji managed to get me into one of those rooms.

The next morning, I went to pay my obeisance to Guru-ji with a basket of fruits as an offering. He blessed me. He was very busy that day; many disciples had come to visit him. He was kind and considerate enough to arrange for a person from the ashram to show me around Rishikesh that afternoon. I was completely taken in by the unique mixture of Hindu devotees and Caucasian yoga practitioners. Some were performing afternoon yoga poses on the banks of the Ganges. I met a group of Dutch devotees, and I spent an interesting hour with them discussing their experiences in Rishikesh. They were there for a six-week yoga course. I asked them rather flippantly, "How do you survive on the strict vegetarian Hindu meals?"

They laughed and told me, "Oh, no, there is a German bakery in town, and that's where we get our breakfast." They walked with me to the German Bakery, where we had strong coffee and afternoon snacks, and I decided then and there that this would be my usual breakfast place in Rishikesh.

My local guide also took me to the place where George Harrison and John Lennon had learned to play the sitar from the famous Indian musician Ravi Shankar. I suddenly remembered my favorite Beatles song, "All You Need Is Love." I was enchanted by the unique blend of Eastern spirituality and the simple pleasures of the Western lifestyle. On one of my visits, I saw a herd of wild elephants, including males, females, and young ones, splashing water on each other with their trunks. It was a rare and magical experience, and I spent more than half an hour watching them from a safe distance on the bank of the Ganges.

My days in Rishikesh started with an early morning bath in the river, followed by a light breakfast at the German Bakery. I would then return to the ashram to join the yoga class that Guru-ji taught there. There were about fifteen students learning yoga from him. After lunch, a few of us would visit the temple of Lord Shiva, up on a hilltop. In the evening, we would have a light vegetarian supper followed by Guru-ji's teaching on the *Gita* for an hour or two.

I went back to Rishikesh at least a half a dozen times, both to meet Guru-ji and because I was so drawn to the city's palpable, unique blend of East and West.

It was there that I learned of the Sivananda Yoga Teaching Center by the Neyyar Dam near Trivandrum, in Kerala. I wanted to visit the center and enroll in their six-week course of yoga teachers' training to go deeper into my practice and learning. If I am honest with myself, I was also drawn to Kerala because of all that I had heard about it, including its rainforest, Ayurvedic massage treatment centers, spectacular beaches, and the unique houseboats that took one down rivers and lagoons.

My six-week residential course at the Sivananda center was enlightening and revelatory. The main textbook on yoga, called Patanjali Sutra, emphasized repeatedly that yoga is not a practice for Hindus only and can be taught to humankind universally. I had read it, but I realized the full amplification of the text at the Sivananda center. The head of the teacher-training center was an Italian, more than six feet tall, who had been sent to Trivandrum from the Sivananda headquarters in Quebec. His deputy was Swami Swarupananda, a white Southern Rhodesian doctor. He told me during my stay at the center that while practicing pediatrics in London, he had passed by an Indian temple. He had been curious about what happened inside, so one morning, before going to work at the hospital, he entered the shrine, where an old wizened South Indian sage looked at him and said, "Oh, I have been waiting for you. Why don't you come and learn yoga from me?"

The doctor was surprised and intrigued. Over a period of six years, he learned the Indian philosophy and practice of yoga from the South Indian priest. He was then sent to the Sivananda center in Quebec before being assigned to be the deputy chief at the center in Kerala. There were many people of different nationalities serving there, and this almost United Nations–like community of yogis showed me another dimension of the global reach of yoga.

One day, I asked the Italian head of the center, "What do you miss most of the western lifestyle in this place?"

He looked into my eyes. "Don't laugh, Satish, but I do miss pizza."

"Swami, you are still bound by your karma," I replied mischievously.

Although I did learn techniques of Hatha yoga, the physical postures and practices, I was more attracted and committed to meditation and its liberating qualities. The Italian swami was an excellent meditation guide. Guru-ji had taught me passages of the *Gita*, and in Kerala, I learned how to read and meditate on Patanjali Sutra. I learned more about the value of karma yoga, or the path of action to help those less privileged and left behind. Mahatma Gandhi also emphasized karma yoga during his movement to liberate India from the British rule. It reminded me of my childhood lessons from Master Sahib Nageshwor, which had included learning to be helpful to those less privileged than I was.

At the end of the six weeks, there was an elaborate ceremony that lasted the whole day. First, we offered incense, a basket of fruit, and two white *dhotis* (traditional garments) to our swami. After accepting our offerings, he blessed us and asked us to choose a personal mantra. There were over a dozen mantras one could choose from. I noticed that many of my colleagues chose "Om Namah Shivaya," a powerful mantra believed to have been given by Lord Shiva to human beings. Some others chose mantras to please Lord Krishna or the Goddess of Knowledge, Saraswathi. When my turn came, I opted for "Om," which as a yogic mantra, is chanted slowly as "A-u-m," emanating from the throat and reaching up the channels of your brain to the top of your head.

Spiritually nurtured and nourished by the tradition of yoga, I returned to Calcutta, where my wife, Sheila, noticed some positive improvements in my outlook on life. I still chant "Om," but to my regret, not every day.

I undertook a couple of pilgrimages with my friend and former colleague Rajagopal Krishna Ram, whom we called Ram. One of the visits took me to the holy city of Sarnath, ten kilometers northeast of Varanasi. After attaining enlightenment, it is believed that Lord Buddha came to Sarnath and gave his first sermon to his five disciples. Decades ago, when Amir had died in Banaras, I had thought a lot about Lord Buddha and his principles on human suffering (*dukkha*) and its causes. After my nephew Niranjan committed suicide, I had visited two famous Buddhist temples near Kathmandu, Swayambhunath and Boudhanath. Later, as a family, Sheila, Sarina, Samir, and I went to visit Lumbini in southwestern Nepal, where Buddha was born as a prince named Siddhartha. I was struck by the peace and quiet of the forest in Lumbini, where Mayadevi, Siddhartha's mother, had given birth to him. The Japanese government and Thai monasteries had invested in a massive rehabilitation and restoration of Lumbini under the auspices of the Lumbini Development Trust.

While in Calcutta, I also came across a most thoughtful book by one of my favorite authors, Pico Iyer, called *The Open Road*. It is the most interpretative biography of the Dalai Lama, with an exceptional introduction to Tibetan Buddhism. Thus, in addition to yoga, I became fascinated by Buddhism and studied its principles and philosophy, especially two texts, the *Heart Sutra* and the *Diamond Sutra*. My forays into yoga, meditation, and the deeper study of Buddhism were perhaps an unconscious, persistent effort to heal from the traumatic experiences of the previous few years and to try to become a better human being.

CHAPTER 31

ADDIS ABABA

THERE was a significant dimension to our family life during our stay in Calcutta. Sarina informed us that she would be posted to Addis Ababa in the near future, and perhaps we could meet her in Addis after she was settled. Sheila and I noted with satisfaction that perhaps it was a connection of karma.

Sheila had helped me by taking notes of my various drafts which I had written for the educational innovative projects in Africa. This was also the first extracurricular work which Sheila and I worked on together, to earn $1,000 U.S. as an honorarium in 1971.

Equally important to us was the memory of an Ethiopian family friend, a beautiful young Ethiopian princess called Atnaf, who was married to my friend Tereffe, my classmate at the Institute of Social Studies from 1965 to 1968. They stayed on in the Netherlands in pursuit of my friend's PhD degree, and returned to Ethiopia after the revolution there. He was appointed as the Minister of Education after his return to his country. Tragically, he was assassinated for his independent ideology, inconsistent with the thinking of the military regime. He was killed when he was fleeing away at night towards the border of Sudan. Nobody knows what happened to Atnaf. She used to appear in Sheila's nightmarish dreams in the Netherlands. When we visited Sarina in Addis Ababa, Sheila went to the most famous church in Addis and offered half a dozen candles in the memory of Atnaf. Sheila believes even now that the nightmares stopped after the offering of the candles in the church.

To me, these looked like karmic connections with Ethiopia. I firmly believed that there was a karmic connection between us, the citizens of the Nepali kingdom, and the tragic death of Atnaf, a princess of the Royal Imperial household in Ethiopia. Since my working there in 1971, there had been a violent revolution in Ethiopia. Many educated elites were killed or forced to flee their homeland, like my two close friends. The revolution, the following famine, and the international efforts to raise funds by celebrities had given me a sense of sorrow about that beautiful country.

We were very happy when we learned that Sarina would be posted by PACT in Addis for a couple of years. This led to two reunions: a reunion of our family, and my reunion with a country I had visited in my youth and had grown to love. Addis Ababa had grown into a more populous, commercial city full of Chinese and Indian business enterprises and booming construction. We traveled around the country, visiting the Rift Valley, lakes, and natural hot springs in Wondo Genet.

Sarina introduced us to a handsome and tall young Ethiopian man, Elias, who was her boyfriend and would later become her husband. One of the most memorable highlights of our stay in Addis Ababa was Sarina and Elias's wedding ceremony, which was held in 2009. The wedding was a unique blend of Hindu religious elements and a traditional Ethiopian Orthodox ceremony. Sheila and I were proud parents, and Elias's family loved us. I remember one of Elias's aunts, a tall woman with a natural grace and a white streak in her hair, who reminded me a lot of Indira Gandhi. The

Nepali side of the family—particularly the ladies—were taken, I noticed, with one of Elias's tall and handsome uncles; the ladies remarked that he could have been in a Hollywood movie.

Sarina's godmother, Ida, had flown in from The Hague to attend the ceremony, and a small group of Nepali family members came from the United States. It was a truly international affair.

PART 3

CHAPTER 32

ON A JOYFUL JOURNEY AGAIN

A FTER seven years in Calcutta, Sheila's oncologist informed us that she was now cancer-free; there was very little chance of a recurrence. She would only require annual checkups. Our whole family celebrated the good news. Samir, who was living in Melbourne, suggested that we join him in Australia. While we were happy and comfortable in Calcutta, so close to Nepal, we were feeling a sense of loneliness due to the distance from our children; one settled in Australia, and the other now in New York. Our close-knit family of four had ended up on three continents! !

We decided to take Samir up on his invitation, and packed our bags once again. Samir had gone back to Monash University to complete his degree in information technology after having worked for several years in Sydney and Canberra.

Australia had always fascinated me as the link nation between the western civilization and the countries of Indo-Pacific region. While teaching in Holland, I had met many Indonesians who looked at Australia as an outpost of British Colonialism, and some

Australians who were somewhat afraid of Indonesian leadership, especially under President Sukarno's radical nationalism, and his stance on non-aligned independent foreign policy.

Australia is a country of natural contrasts, with exotic wildlife such as koalas, kangaroos, and crocodiles. It offers oceanic beauty, such as multi-colored reefs under the ocean, lovely beaches, and hundreds of locations for swimming and surfing. I was pleasantly surprised by the urban setting and design of Melbourne on the Yarra River. Though Australia is 500 times larger than Nepal in geographical terms, it had much less population in 2009. During my morning walks in Melbourne, I was surprised to see more cars than people on the street. I liked the laid-back lifestyle I observed among Australians, and their socially responsible model of healthcare. I remembered George Bernard Shaw's famous saying, that Great Britain and the United States were two countries separated by a common language. I thought to myself, if Shaw had been to Australia, he would have added a third country. Our time in the culturally rich city of Melbourne gave us a good deal of satisfaction and joy.

Sheila and I flew to Melbourne with great anticipation of meeting Samir. My mind went back to different strands of memories, related to Samir's journey to Australia for further studies in 1996. I remembered that I too was very unhappy to leave my father and mother while going to Banaras. Samir was similarly reluctant about going to Australia. He was very close to his mother, and did not want to go alone, leaving her behind in Nepal. During the flight from Calcutta to Melbourne, I realized that his adamant refusal to go to Australia was rooted in his concern at leaving his mother behind. It had taken a good deal of persuasion by my friend, the then-Australian Ambassador, and me to convince him to sign the visa-related documents.

My colleague, Professor Joop Syataw, had often encouraged me to visit the state of Victoria in Australia. He often praised that state as the most beautiful part of the Aussie Federation, with alpine weather and plants in the upper elevations, and almost

Mediterranean beaches around the seashore. When we landed at the Melbourne International Airport, two things struck me immediately: one, how neat, clean, and spacious it was, compared with the crowded airport of Calcutta, and, secondly, the porters at the airport flatly refused to accept tips. Having flown within the United States, where tips are considered to be part of the income, and having lived in India, where the porters jostle with each other and compete like wrestlers to carry the luggage, this was a novel experience.

The river Yarra along the highway to Samir's residence reminded me of the Ganges, on one hand, and the Rhine in Europe, on the other. I was pleasantly surprised by the urban setting and design of Melbourne on the Yarra River.

I was always attracted to the city of Melbourne from the point of view of urban planning. It is admired throughout Asia for its unique blend of European classical architecture, with functional, utilitarian American design for skyscrapers, malls, and shopping centers.

Flinders Street was the heart of city, and it is often compared with downtown Manhattan. The spacious and elegant Federation Square is pleasing to the eye, and comfortable to the feet of visitors. The hop-on, hop-off bus and tram provides easy transport to young and old alike. Sheila and I used them frequently to move around the city.

Often, we frequented the National Gallery of Victoria, which has one of the largest collections of Australian and European paintings. This gallery reminded me of the Rijksmuseum in Amsterdam. Melbourne also has the Immigration Museum, which is particularly refreshing in a time when national borders are increasingly being closed, and people are shut out instead of welcomed. Vivid displays celebrate the people coming to Australia from Britain, Italy, Greece, Vietnam, and China.

The diversity of the people and cultures is remarkable in Melbourne. We learned that Melbourne has the largest number of Greeks outside of Greece. There is even a Greek-language daily newspaper. The mayor of Melbourne was one Mr. So, a prominent Australian of Chinese origin. Indians, Pakistanis, and Vietnamese people also contribute to the cultural flavor of the metropolis.

One of my proudest memories in Melbourne consists of the unforgettable evening at Monash University. Samir, together with other students, was being awarded a degree in information technology. I had pressed Samir to study in Australia, since Monash University is globally renowned for its excellence in the fields of information technology and computational sciences.

During the convocation address, the Vice-Chancellor of Monash University referred to a memorable paragraph from a well-known Russian novelist, Vasily Grossman, one of my favorite novelists, whose book I still have in my apartment in Manhattan.

There was another milestone in the life of Prabasi clan. It involved Samir's marriage to Nidhi Rana, a Nepali girl who studied and lived in Sydney for many years. It called for a family union and celebration. Sarina's family, i.e., Elias, Sarina, and our little grand-daughter Junu flew over from Addis Ababa to Melbourne. The marriage ceremony was held in an impressive South Indian temple of Lord Shiva. That evening, we had a festive party with drinks and dinner, with the participation of Samir's friends from Sydney and Canberra, and Nidhi's friends from Sydney. It was a night to remember.

CHAPTER 33
THE UNITED STATES: LAND OF LIBERTY AND SUFFERING

Sᴏᴍᴇᴛɪᴍᴇs in human life, small events lead to unforeseen consequences. Sheila and I traveled from Melbourne to New York to visit our grandchildren and spend some time with them. Sarina and Elias's children—Junu, the elder, and Munu, the younger— were the apples of our eyes. As new grandparents, Sheila and I were so happy to be with them that we didn't realize how quickly time had flown.

The New York of 2010 is so different from the New York I had visited during my UN days. I remember my first visit to New York, as UNICEF Regional Planning Officer, at the end of 1976. I stayed at the popular, UN-patronized hotel called Doral Inn on Third Avenue. Abraham Beame was the mayor of the city then. My friend Mr. Ramon Harmano of UNICEF came to my hotel for a nightcap. I asked him for his advice about moving around New York. He gave me lots of tips, among which I remember even now two major points. He said, "Satish, in the evening, after 7 pm, you should not walk very close to the walls of the buildings.

There may be danger lurking there. Secondly, always walk to the lighted side of the street and also be on the lookout for dog shit on the street." I told him that coming from Nepal, I know about the dog shit, but what about the other two points. He said that there is a lot of stabbing and wallet snatching. There was rampant crime on the street at night.

Since then, New York has improved in some respects, and deteriorated in others. I have visited New York during the terms of four mayors, including Mr. Beame. He was followed by Ed Koch, and then Rudy Giuliani, and currently Mr. Bill de Blasio. Koch made the city much more livable with cultural diversity. He was very popular among average New Yorkers as well as millionaires. Giuliani was the mayor of the city during the momentous episode of 9/11, followed by terrible events of revenge against Muslims and immigrants in general. Mr. de Blasio, as a Democrat, is trying to re-establish a sense of balance in city administration, while trying to protect New Yorkers from the anti-poor policies of the current federal administration.

Sarina, in her own meticulous way, had other plans for us. She extended our tourist visa. Sheila and I felt that Elias and Sarina needed family support to look after their young kids. Both were full-time professionals who were overextended in terms of time. Sarina had a leadership role at the international nonprofit WaterAid, while Elias was busy with extending his Ethiopian coffee business, Buunni Coffee.

We settled down after what we hoped would be our final move, from Melbourne to New York, in 2014. We also encouraged Samir and his wife, Nidhi, to consider moving to the United States. As both were Australian citizens, it would not be difficult for them to find employment in the U.S. We were tired of living on different continents, and wanted to have the normalcy of a family routine where we could easily visit each other and we could be together with our children and grandchildren.

Sheila and I now live a quiet life in Upper Manhattan, in a peaceful neighborhood with parks and playgrounds. Above all, we have the pleasure of being able to walk to Sarina and Elias's apartment and play with our grandchildren, our most profound source of satisfaction and joy. Both Junu and Munu attended preschool across the street from our apartment. On many an afternoon, we would pick them up after school and bring them over to our apartment. Snacks and giggle-filled fun would ensue, and as grandparents, Sheila and I continue to get immense pleasure from the time we spend with the girls.

I am reminded of the circle of life as I take my granddaughters to the library and nurture in them a love of books and learning. I can already see that they are becoming the next generation of booklovers like me. I am deeply touched now, when I see that statue of Lord Buddha on Sarina's bookshelf. I hope one day she will pass it on to our eldest granddaughter, Junu, when she leaves home to go to college.

My spiritual guide Guru-ji had emphasized to all his disciples that one must choose a location for meditation and yoga. Citing Sanskrit scriptures, he emphasized the importance of selecting a place with three attributes. One, it should be a place where one can gaze at the blueness of the unending sky. Two, it should be surrounded by a canopy of tall trees that do not hinder the view up above. Three, it should be near a source of flowing water. To my great delight, Linden Terrace at Fort Tryon Park in Upper Manhattan offered just such a location. In this highest part of Manhattan, I can sit on a bench under open sky, overlooking the mighty Hudson River, surrounded by a canopy of trees stretching into the distance. Depending on the weather, I can sit in this spot for an hour or so, meditating on my past life, and possible approaches to higher levels of consciousness.

Fort Tryon Park is a delight to visit in every season. The carpet of seasonal flowers in bloom along the pathways and the low-hanging branches of flowering trees offer additional visual pleasures. Senior citizens taking in the rays of the early spring sun, young and vivacious couples vigorously jogging with their dogs, expectant mothers walking in thoughtful solitude, and young children scampering ahead of their parents—these are the sights I am taken with on my walks in the park.

Above all, from the days of early fall stretching into the winter, I admire the beauty, and reflect on the significance of falling leaves in a garden which regenerates itself. Sometimes it leads me to hum "What a Wonderful World." Sometimes I feel anguished as to how we are so capable of inciting violence in our lives, by neglecting the natural world, our precious blue planet, without realizing the fragility of life and the consequences of greed.

CHAPTER 34

THE MUSIC OF THE FALLING
LEAVES: SOME REFLECTIONS

Softly, deftly, music shall caress you
Hear it, feel it, secretly possess you.
—CHARLES HART

I AM BLESSED, to have lived and led a remarkably satisfying life. In the autumn years of my life, I am often struck by the interplay between the march of history and the role of individuals in influencing and shaping it. I still ponder the question, "What if?" What if someone had not killed the Duke of Sarajevo? What if someone had arrested and imprisoned Vladimir Lenin before he returned to St. Petersburg from Germany? What if Lord Mountbatten had not, in a rush to judgment, divided the Indian sub-continent along religious lines?

In addition to these questions about the consequences of an individual's action on the mass of humanity, I ponder the question of values in one's own life. I become melancholy at society's emerging tendencies towards self-destruction. My greatest source of sorrow is the trend to becoming completely absorbed by the internet, at a high cost of disconnecting from our "inner-net" moral values, civic sense, and an instinctive feeling of what is right and what is wrong. We seem to be moving at great speed and even greater expediency into a future where the acquisition of wealth, coupled with fifteen minutes of fame, is leading us astray, stifling questions of morality, ethics, and the purpose of life.

There are six emerging trends that are particularly striking to me. First, the liberal global order's struggle against the emergence of illiberal waves; second, the growing Janus-like impact of technology; third, the environmental and ecological imbalance leading to global disaster; fourth, the increasing homogenization of the world; fifth, over-consumption of resources; and sixth, skewed population growth, leading to inequality and immigration from the poor to the rich countries, and consequent violence.

Ever since the Renaissance in Europe, some five centuries ago, human beings have been attracted to liberal values rooted in individual choice and individual freedoms. I myself have been enchanted by this European philosophy. I observe an emerging belief that sons of heaven must dominate others to establish a global social order. Inheritors of the world of the Byzantine emperors, the Czars, and the adherents of Confucius are redefining the global order. It is a deeply worrying trend and raises big questions in my mind about where we are headed.

As a student of history, I have learned a few lessons from the rise and fall of civilizations. There are the instances of the rise and fall of the ancient Chinese Kingdoms, the Assyrian and Egyptian civilizations, the glory and decay of the Jewish empire, and the Inca civilization in South America, which all show a pattern of achievement and decline.

I was fascinated by the appearance of a typewriter when I was studying in Banaras. I could not afford to buy it, but its elegance and the speed with which one could write enticed me. From the relative simplicity and elegance of the typewriter, we have moved

now to interconnected, data-driven, algorithm-based technolog-
ical miracles, which are frightening in their capacity to control
us. In Hinduism, we believe in three gods: the creator, the protector, and the destroyer. The three global gurus of technology,
Alphabet (Google's parent company), Amazon, and Facebook,
have become our new gods of creation, preservation, domination
and destruction. This has resulted in one aggrieved superpower
trying to dethrone another, using new forms of cyberwarfare.

I have seen the world move toward cultural homogenization to
such an extent that the curiosity and pleasure of discovering the
new in other lands, cultures, and peoples is disappearing. In my
early days of traveling, I was delighted by the specialties, unique
features, flavors, and colors of each place that I visited. Now, I
see sameness in shopping centers, clothing styles, and even food
and drink at opposite ends of the earth. There is a dullness and
a lack of imagination evident in this trend that is truly depress-
ing. Tourism, which has been a means of individual experience,
growth, and learning, has become more about the mass consump-
tion of distorted versions of other cultures. I am grieved to learn
from the newspapers that my beloved city of Amsterdam has put
strict restrictions on the number of tours and tour guides visiting
Canal Street and the Red Light District at night.

We focus on the scissor-like sharpness of the market forces
of supply and demand, and have completely forgotten the moral
and philosophical basis for human uplift and economic progress.
Manipulation of the market by supersized companies has distorted the markets. The prime example of this is the dominance
over the book trade by Amazon, leading to the closure and disappearance of dozens of independent book stores.

Most frightening of all is our headlong rush toward the
destruction of the only earth we have, the home that has helped
human existence as well as sustenance. Hindu scriptures teach
us that after waking up in the morning and before setting our
feet on the ground, we should apologize to Mother Earth for the
pain that we cause to her by our weight. There are innumerable

examples of our greed destroying future life on Earth. Walden Pond, where Henry David Thoreau famously wrote his reflection on life and nature, is increasingly filled with phosphorus. The source of this contamination is human urination around the pond resulting from the celebrated site's large number of visitors. Even in our appreciation of nature, we are not thinking about the consequences of our seemingly trivial acts. The rapid degradation of our ecology, our water, and our climate is humanity's biggest existential threat.

I remember that Sir Edmund Hillary of New Zealand, and Tenzing Norgay, a legendary Sherpa from Nepal, were the first to climb the summit of Mount Everest, the tallest mountain range on earth. Thanks to their accomplishment, the land of Gurkhas gradually became known as "the land of Sherpas." A recent research study conducted by Swiss and other European scientists has concluded that the vanishing glaciers and the melting snow over the mountain ranges surrounding Mount Everest will decrease by one-third in the next 30 years. The unforeseen consequences of the melting snow is that the decomposed bodies of mountaineers who disappeared decades ago are becoming visible, and Tibetan vultures have begun to feed on the emerging cadavers. A solid consequence is that employment and income in the northeastern region of Nepal has begun to decline, leading to unhappiness among the Sherpas. For instance, people living in and around Namche Bazaar have begun to look for new avenues of income.

There is also a wasteful tendency towards overconsumption, with the result that human beings gobble up as many resources as possible. A recent table published in the weekly British magazine *The Economist* shows the use of drinking water in the production of some of the consumable items popular with urban dwellers.

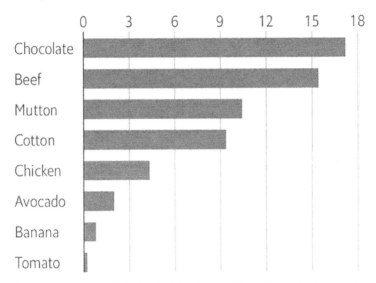

The worst for thirst
Volume of water required to produce 1kg
2010, litres '000

Sources: Institute of Mechanical Engineers; Water Footprint Network
The Economist

These harmful tendencies, the results of which we will not know in the foreseeable future, are a cause for concern for all of us. While visiting Fort Tryon Park, I carry and reread a thoughtful portion from a small book called *The Powerful Good Wish*. I am especially struck by the message given by Buddha and his disciples, "Listen! All apparent Being, whether of the Round or of Deliverance, is in Principle One with two paths and two fruits. This is the jugglery of Ignorance and Knowledge. By the good wish of the Altogether Good One, may all, entering the royal abode of the Divine Essence, manifestly and completely attain to Buddha-hood."

Our resolution to choose between the path of Ignorance and the path of Knowledge will determine the kind of fruit we harvest.

In this age of abundance, we seem to be perpetually unhappy. The half-full glass always appears half-empty to us. Rome burned because of Nero's excessive love of the music of the lute. I see parallels in this land of liberty and compassion, where the game of golf and other addictive passions are leading us to possible destruction. The North American preoccupation with entertainment through all means and its headlong rush to *Sex in the City* have distorted the very foundational values on which the democratic tradition of this country was built.

The noble goal of the American Constitution, guaranteeing life, liberty, and the pursuit of happiness, has been tarnished by the amendments attached to it. It would be amusing if it was not so tragic to reflect upon the ignorance of many Americans of their own Constitution, while being completely preoccupied with the amendments to it.

The United States of America, the republic founded on the quest for liberty and committed to the promotion of democracy all over the world, has been, in my view, subverted by political donors, industries, and lobbyists who would manipulate democratic process for personal gain. *Dark Money*, by Jane Mayer, has eloquently expressed the mechanism through which it influences the legislative processes in Congress. I am equally disturbed by the global disequilibrium affecting humanity. There is a Chinese saying, "May you live in interesting times"—this is both a blessing and a curse. We are living through interesting times, indeed.

I am encouraged by the younger generation in the United States, but I am frustrated by the shackles placed around them to prevent them from choosing a noble path. I am encouraged by the Anglo-Saxon heritage and track record of muddling through, but I am disturbed by their sensationalist tendencies, abetted by the 24/7 highlights of inanity called news. According to the New York Times, a major portion of the American population does not remember the reason for invading Vietnam, nor the rationale for the Iraq War.

The loss of historical memory is the most significant and evil tendency emerging in this exceptional country. I am encouraged by the new swell of young people who think globally and are trying to act locally. I take heart from the music of my university days in Britain. Beatlemania afflicted me along with the rest of the island, and then the world.

Throughout my life I have taken great pleasure in playing with children. I remember my nieces and nephews in Banaras with great fondness. The death of Amir, with whom I used to play in the household of my dear sister Satyawati, led to a momentous change in me. I changed my name by adding Prabasi to it, and the burning ghats of Banaras instilled in me a different attitude towards life, living and death. Perhaps it also led to my preference for working with UNICEF, so that untimely and unnatural deaths of children like Amir could be reduced in the future.

Playing with my two grandchildren gives me joy as well as speculative worries with wistful reflections on the future of mankind. I take the eldest one to the New York Public Library (NYPL), where she picks up loads of books, almost equivalent to her weight. The younger one is a bubbling, smiling, somewhat naughty bundle of energy. I often play with them in Fort Tryon Park, and imagine different scenarios as to what kind of planet they are going to inherit. Will it be an uninhabitable earth, or a place of perpetual sunshine and unending happiness?

My own life has been influenced by three myths. First is the Greek myth of Sisyphus. He tried to lift a heavy stone towards the heaven, hoping that he could reach the Temple of God. Every time he fell down, because of a curse, he would get up, and try again, but to no avail. The endeavor of human beings to reach perfection reminds me of the persistent Sisyphean struggle; we lift the load and yet fall down at each endeavor.

Secondly, I have been influenced by the Hindu story of Eklavya, described in the *Mahabharata*. A poor but exceptionally talented student named Eklavya was keen to master the art of archery. Due to his lowly caste origins, the guru named Dronacharya could not accept him as his student. Undaunted, Eklavya carved out a statue of the guru and practiced archery alone for many years. Over the years he excelled in his skills and defeated all the archers in the land. When the guru found about this, he asked, in keeping with the Hindu tradition, *gurudakshi-na*—a gift for the teacher.

Eklavya was happy that the guru appreciated his skills and asked the guru to name a gift. The guru asked for the thumb of Eklavya's right hand. Eklavya paused for only a moment before cutting off his thumb as a gift to his teacher. This story reminds me of the treachery imposed by the caste system in South Asia, and the human capacity to indulge in acts of inequality by fair or foul means. When I read about voter suppression in this land of liberty, inequal treatment of citizens of different races, and economic dominance by less than one percent of population over more than 99 percent of U.S. citizens, I am reminded of my ancient friend Eklavya.

My teachers and thought-guru, Lord Buddha and Jesus Christ, asserted the perfectibility of man, insisting that human beings could become more perfect, more godly. In fact, the name Buddha denotes enlightenment — human beings becoming more perfect. Though dark clouds hover over humankind in the first quarter of the twenty-first century, I strongly believe that we will overcome our self-inflicted obstacles and wounds. I take heart in Shelley's memorable poem, "Ode to the West Wind," which asserts in one of the stanzas, "Can spring be far behind?"

In order to get away from these dark thoughts about human existence, I begin to hum the Beatle's famous song, "All You Need is Love." My youngest grandchild, Munu, teases me by saying, "Baba daddy, you don't know how to sing." That brings a wistful smile to my lips.

HIGHLY ABRIDGED LIST
OF BOOKS

My life has revolved around hundreds of books, in fact books have been a nutritional input to my life. The books listed below are a selection of titles that have deeply impacted me.

List A
Quotations sources
Page 19. Mark Twain, *Following the Equator*, p. 480.

Page 39. Sylvain Levi, *A Notebook of Sojourn*, p. 35.

Page 66. Martin Haug, trans. *The Atreya Brahmanam of the Rig Veda*, 7.15.

Page 136: Mark Roskill, editor, *The Letters of Vincent Van Gogh*.

Page 166: Paul T.K. Lin with Eileen Chen Lin, *In the Eye of the China Storm: A life Between East and West.*

Page 314: W. Somerset Maugham, *Of Human Bondage*

Page 393: Marco Pallis, *Peaks and Lamas*

"A Mighty Purpose: How Jim Grant Sold the World on Saving its Children" by Adam Fifield, Reviewed by Helen Epstein, *New York Review of Books.*

Page 87: *The Post American World,* by Fareed Zakaria

List B

Books read in childhood

- A Nepali book of myths and stories called *Sunkeshari Maiya ko Katha* (Stories of the lady with golden hair)

- *Nala Ra Damyanti ko Katha* (Historic tale of a man called Nala and a lady called Damyanti)

- Various stories of Lord Rama, Krishna, and Buddha

Books read during college years

- *Autobiography of an Unknown Indian* by Nirad C. Chaudhuri

- *Discovery of India* by Jawaharlal Nehru

- *The Quest for the Origins of Vedic Culture* by Edwin Bryant

- *An Area of Darkness* by V.S. Naipaul

- *The Idea of India* by Sunil Khilnani

- *Lost Masters: The Sages of Ancient Greece* by Linda Johnson

- Many books by progressive Indian authors who wrote in Hindi language, notable among them is *From Volga to Ganges* by Rahul Sankrityayan.

Books read during European sojourn

Fiction

- *A Tale of Two Cities* by Charles Dickens

- *Pride and Prejudice* by Jane Austin

- *Anna Karenina* by Leo Tolstoy

- *Crime and Punishment* by Fyodor Dostoevsky

- *The Brothers Karamazov* by Fyodor Dostoevsky

- *The Double* by Fyodor Dostoevsky

- *Doctor Zhivago* by Boris Pasternak
- *The Good Earth* by Pearl S. Buck
- *The Plague* by Albert Camus
- *The Stranger (L' Etranger)* by Albert Camus
- *Animal Farm* by George Orwell
- *1984* by George Orwell
- *The Mountain is Young* by Han Suyin
- *The Razor's Edge* by Somerset Maugham

Nonfiction

- *A Dying Colonialism* by Frantz Fanon
- *The Wretched of the Earth* by Frantz Fanon
- *Revolution in the Revolution?* by Regis Debray
- *My Half Century: Selected Prose by Anna Akhmatova*
- *The Travels* by Marco Polo
- *A Record of Buddhist Kingdoms: An Account of Chinese Monk Fâ-Hien of his travels in India and Ceylon*
- *Chinese Thought: From Confucius to Mao Tse-Tung* by H.G.Creel
- *Ancient Chinese Thought: Modern Chinese Power* by Nyan Xuetong
- *Chinese Shadows* by Simon Leys
- *1968: The Year that Rocked the World* by Mark Kurlansky
- *The Best and the Brightest* by David Halberstam
- *No Ordinary Time* by Doris K Goodwin
- *Scoundrel Time* by Lillian Hellman
- *Writing Dangerously: Mary McCarthy and Her World* by Carol Brightman

- *A People's History of the United States* by Howard Zinn

- *Howard Zinn speaks: Collected speeches 1963-2009* by Howard Zinn

- *Reappraisals: Reflections on the Forgotten Twentieth Century* by Tony Judt

- *Christ Stopped at Eboli* by Carlo Levi

- *What Fanon Said: A Philosophical Introduction to His Life and Thought* by Lewis Gordon

Travelogues and Memoirs

- *Travels with Charley in Search of America* by John Steinbeck

- *The Open Road: the Global Journey of the Fourteenth Dalai Lama* by Pico Iyer

- *The Lady and the Monk: Four Seasons in Kyoto* by Pico Iyer

- *The Art of Stillness: Adventures in Going Nowhere* by Pico Iyer

- *The World of Yesterday* by Stefan Zweig

- *Down and Out in Paris and London* by George Orwell

- *Homage to Catalonia* by George Orwell

- *The Burmese Days* by George Orwell